teach®
yourself

**brazilian
portuguese**

brazilian
portuguese
sue tyson-ward

For over 60 years, more than
40 million people have learnt over
750 subjects the **teach yourself**
way, with impressive results.

be where you want to be
with **teach yourself**

Dedication
For Mum and Dad

For UK order enquiries: please contact Bookpoint Ltd, 130 Milton Park, Abingdon, Oxon OX14 4SB. Telephone: +44 (0) 1235 827720. Fax: +44 (0) 1235 400454. Lines are open 09.00–17.00, Monday to Saturday, with a 24-hour message answering service. Details about our titles and how to order are available at www.teachyourself.co.uk

For USA order enquiries: please contact McGraw-Hill Customer Services, PO Box 545, Blacklick, OH 43004-0545, USA. Telephone: 1-800-722-4726. Fax: 1-614-755-5645.

For Canada order enquiries: please contact McGraw-Hill Ryerson Ltd, 300 Water St, Whitby, Ontario L1N 9B6, Canada. Telephone: 905 430 5000. Fax: 905 430 5020.

Long renowned as the authoritative source for self-guided learning – with more than 40 million copies sold worldwide – the **teach yourself** series includes over 300 titles in the fields of languages, crafts, hobbies, business, computing and education.

British Library Cataloguing in Publication Data: a catalogue record for this title is available from the British Library.

Library of Congress Catalog Card Number: on file.

First published in UK 1997 by Hodder Education, 338 Euston Road, London, NW1 3BH.

First published in US 1997 by The McGraw-Hill Companies, Inc.

This edition published 2003.

The **teach yourself** name is a registered trade mark of Hodder Headline.

Typeset by Transet Limited, Coventry, England.
Printed in Great Britain for Hodder Education, a division of Hodder Headline, 338 Euston Road, London, NW1 3BH, by Cox & Wyman Ltd, Reading, Berkshire.

Hodder Headline's policy is to use papers that are natural, renewable and recyclable products and made from wood grown in sustainable forests. The logging and manufacturing processes are expected to conform to the environmental regulations of the country of origin.

Impression number   15 14 13 12 11 10
Year   2009 2008 2007 2006

contents

This course is designed for the absolute beginner and requires no previous knowledge of any foreign language. The aim of the course is to enable you to use Brazilian Portuguese in everyday situations and also to provide some background information about Brazil and Brazilian culture.

The Portuguese of Brazil is different from that of Continental Portugal in three main ways: vocabulary, grammatical structures, and, most importantly, pronunciation. You could consider the two variants of the language in the same way as American and British English. It is widely considered that Brazilian Portuguese is actually easier to understand than European, as the Portuguese speak very quickly, with their mouths closed very much around the words, and they often 'eat' the beginning and ending of words. If you are learning Brazilian Portuguese, be assured that people will understand what you are saying (apart from the odd few words) throughout the Portuguese-speaking world. It is important for you to understand that you are learning not 'Brazilian', but 'Brazilian Portuguese'. It is surprising how many people (including some native speakers) believe 'Brazilian' is actually a language. It is not; it is a *variant* of the Portuguese language.

Portuguese is not a difficult language to take on board if you have had some experience of another Latin-based (or Romance) language, such as French, Spanish or Italian. Pronunciation is the main area you will need to concentrate on. Many people erroneously believe that, as it looks like Spanish, it will sound that way too. Constant practice with the recording will help you improve in this respect. If you have no knowledge of a Romance language, or in fact, of *any* language, take heart – you are starting out with a clean slate and with no preconceptions which could mislead you.

The American influence on Brazil, via TV and other mass-media communications has resulted in various English words entering the Brazilian speaker's vocabulary; words such as *shopping*, *flat* and *short* (*shorts*) are commonplace today.

How to use this book

Each of the 18 units is structured as follows:

Introduction. An introduction in English that explains what you will learn in the unit.

Dialogue. There are dialogues at the beginning of each chapter, and sometimes later on. Using the recording (where the symbol appears), listen to them first to check the pronunciation and see how much you understand, then read them carefully, and if necessary, listen again.

Vocabulary. The vocabulary section that follows each dialogue contains the new words and expressions that you will need to understand it.

True or false? These are statements about the texts in either English or Portuguese that may be *true* or *false*. The aim of these exercises is to check whether you have understood the text.

i **Cultural tips:** Hints or tips – comments on life and society as well as background information on Brazil.

Summary. The important words and expressions used in the dialogues are repeated here.

Grammar. Notes explaining grammatical structures and how to create your own sentences.

Exercises/Practices. In these you practise the new words and information you have learnt.

Do you understand? Further dialogues and texts, testing your comprehension. These are not designed to test every word, but to give you the opportunity to 'get the gist' of a text.

The symbol **▶** indicates material included on the accompanying recording.

The best way to make progress is to work a little every day. Listen to the recording and read the dialogues several times, learning the vocabulary before you start the exercises. Try to devise interesting ways to memorize the new words, such as through picture-images, songs, rhymes, etc.

Teach Yourself Brazilian Portuguese follows the journey of Sylvia Peters on a 6-month trip to Brazil, as she endeavours to make social, cultural and business links for future exchange. During the course of her journey you, like her, will visit some of Brazil's most important cities, and be introduced to its people, history and culture. Initially, Sylvia will be the guest of the Ferreira family; José is a marine biologist, and Marli teaches Portuguese in a language school. Sylvia returns to their house before leaving Brazil for the UK.

Acknowledgements

Many thanks to Mrs Lúcia Cooper for materials and guidance and, as ever, to Sarah Mitchell at Hodder for her total encouragement. Thanks, also, to Ginny Catmur at Hodder, for her work on this new edition. And to Brazil, for instilling the fire of life. Viva!

Although this book can successfully be used on its own, the purchase of the recording will enhance both your pronunciation and your comprehension abilities as well as giving you the opportunity for aural revision.

▶ In native Portuguese words there is no **k**, **w**, or **y**, although they appear in imported words. Pronunciation in Brazil varies from region to region, as it may do in any country. There are certain distinct sounds in Rio which mark the speaker as a 'Carioca' (a native of Rio), e.g. the **de** sound at the end of a word pronounced as **gee**.

The whole Portuguese alphabet is as follows. If you have the recording, listen to how it sounds when recited in Portuguese.

a b c d e f g h i j (k) l m n o p q
r s t u v (w) x (y) z

Portuguese vowels

Portuguese vowel sounds are tricky to imitate, as there are nasal sounds, and sounds differ depending on where the vowel is in any given word. However, Brazilians do open their mouths wider than the Portuguese, and are therefore theoretically easier to understand! Here is a general idea:

a, as in *rather* – **falar**   or as in *abide* – **mesa**
ã, as in *rang* – **irmã**.   This is a nasal sound.
e, as in *bell* – **certo**   or as in *madden* – **pesar**
i, as in *mean* – **partida**   or as in *cigar* – **emigrar**
o, as in *saw* – **nova**   or as in *boot* – **sapato**
u, as in *boot* – **durmo**   or as in *bull* – **mudar**

Portuguese consonants

Portuguese consonants also differ from the English sounds in different situations. Follow the table on the recording, if you have it, as each consonant is given an English equivalent, and a Portuguese example:

Consonant	English sound	Portuguese sound
b	*ball*	bonito
c+e/i, ç	*sat*	cem, começa
c+a/o/u	*can*	comer
ch	*shout*	chocolate
d	*dabl'gee'*	dar or cidade
f	*fun*	falar
g + e/i	*pleasure*	geléia
g + a/o/u	*got*	pagar
h	'silent'	hotel
j	*pleasure*	julho
l	*last*	livre/total
lh	*billion*	mulher
m	*map*	mesa
n	*nod*	nadar
nh	*onion*	vinho
p	*pin*	parar
q(u)	*quart*	quando
q(u) + e/i	'silent u'	quem
r (initial)	'aspirated'	rio
r	*ran*	compram
s	*sat*	sol
s + vowels	*zoo*	casa
t	*tap*	todo
v	'as in English'	vida
x	*shout*	baixa
z	*zoo/shout*	fazer

The stress rules

In basic terms, Portuguese words are stressed (i.e. emphasized when spoken) on the last syllable if they end in i, u, groups of two vowels (diphthongs), consonants and nasal vowels, e.g. **papel**, **irmão**.

They are stressed on the syllable before last if they are verbs ending in **am** or **em**, or words ending in **a, e, o, em, ens – mesa, falam**.

If a word breaks either of these rules, a written accent is added to show where the stress falls. So if you see a word with a written accent, you must stress the syllable where the accent is placed.

A few tips to help you acquire an authentic accent

It is not absolutely vital to acquire a perfect accent. The aim is to be understood; here are a number of techniques for working on your pronunciation:

1 Listen carefully to the recording or a native speaker or teacher. Whenever possible repeat aloud imagining you are a native speaker of Portuguese.
2 Tape record yourself and compare your pronunciation with that of a native speaker.
3 Ask native speakers to listen to your pronunciation and tell you how to improve it.
4 Ask native speakers how a specific sound is formed. Watch them and practise at home in front of a mirror.
5 Make a list of words that give you pronunciation trouble and practise them.

01

seu passaporte, por favor
your passport, please

In this unit you will learn
- how to identify people
- how to introduce yourself and address people
- how to say hello and goodbye
- how to check into your hotel

▶ Dialogue 1

Sylvia Peters arrives in Brazil and passes through Customs (**Alfândega**).

Inspetor	Bom dia. Seu passaporte, por favor.
Sylvia	Aqui está.
Inspetor	Você é inglesa, não é?
Sylvia	Sim, sou.
Inspetor	Muito bem. Quanto tempo vai passar aqui?
Sylvia	Seis meses.
Inspetor	Está bem. Obrigado. Tchau.
Sylvia	Bom dia, obrigada.

bom dia	*hello, good morning*	**aqui, cá**	*here*
	(also goodbye)	**está**	*(it) is*
seu	*your*	**você**	*you*
passaporte (o)	*passport*	**é**	*is/are*
por favor	*please*	**inglesa**	*English* (woman)
não é?	*isn't it/is that so?*	**tempo (o)**	*time*
não	*no, not*	**seis**	*six*
sim	*yes*	**meses (os)**	*months*
sou	*I am*	**está bem**	*OK*
muito bem	*very well*	**obrigado/a**	*thank you*
vai passar	*you're going to spend*	**tchau**	*see you/bye*
quanto?	*how much?*		

True or false?

Tick true (*verdadeiro*) or false (*falso*) for the following statements based on the dialogue.

	V	F

a Sylvia Peters is American.
b She's going to spend six weeks in Brazil.
c She arrives in the morning.

Grammar

To be

In Portuguese there are two verbs both meaning **to be**:

Ser is used for permanent characteristics, such as nationality. **Estar** is used more for temporary states and locations.

In the dialogue you saw examples of both verbs:

aqui está	*here it is*	estar
você é inglesa	*you are English*	ser
sim, sou	*yes, I am*	ser
está bem	*that's OK*	estar

You will come across more examples, and find out other ways in which the verbs are used, as you work through the units.

Forms of address: *você*

In Brazil, most people call each other *you* using the word **você**. However, there are certain situations where more, or less, formality in address is called for. Look at the table below to see how these differences work.

Situation	Formal 'you'	Informal 'you'
With strangers, people in higher social/work position	**o senhor** (to man) **a senhora** (to woman)	
With friends, colleagues, family		**você/ tu** (some parts of Brazil)
With older people	**o senhor/a senhora**	

Você and **tu** are examples of what are called *personal pronouns* – the words for *I, you, he,* etc.

Personal pronouns

The Portuguese personal pronouns are used to denote which person is carrying out the action of a verb. They are:

eu	*I*	nós	*we*
(tu)	*you* [used only in some parts of Brazil]		
ele	*he/it*	eles	*they (male)*
ela	*she/it*	elas	*they (female)*
você	*you*	vocês	*you (plural)*

These are referred to as *subject pronouns*, but they are not necessarily used all the time; in many instances the endings of the verbs will suffice to tell you who is doing the action. In the dialogue you had:

| é inglesa | *you are English* |
| sim, sou | *yes, I am* |

You will learn more of verbs later on.

Male/female

In Portuguese, everything you see around you is divided into two groups: masculine and feminine. This is because Portuguese is a language with its roots in Latin, and the Romans used a language system based on words linking together, usually in a logical way (although it may not seem so to many learners!). So, for example, *table* happens to be a feminine word, and *floor* is a masculine one. In most cases you can tell which group a word belongs to by its ending: an -o for masculine words, and an -a for feminine ones, although this is not always the case. A dictionary will guide you when you are first learning, and look for help in the vocabulary lists, until you start to get a feel for the different endings.

Obrigado/a

You will have noticed in the dialogue that the Customs official says **Obrigado**, and Sylvia replies **Obrigada**, both meaning *Thank you*. All men should use the first and women the second, regardless of whom they are addressing. This is because *Obrigado* is an adjective – a word of description, which is applied to the person expressing their gratitude – as in the outdated English *(I am) much obliged*. Another adjective you came across was **inglesa** (*English woman*). The masculine is **inglês** (*English man*).

▶ Dialogue 2

Sylvia arrives and checks in at the hotel where she will be staying before going to the Ferreira home.

| Sylvia | Boa tarde. Sou Sylvia Peters. Tem um apartamento reservado em meu nome? |
| Recepcionista | Um momento. Como se escreve seu sobrenome? |

Sylvia	P-e-t-e-r-s. Peters.
Recepcionista	Ah, sim, aqui está. A senhora Peters, de Manchester.
Sylvia	Isso.
Recepcionista	Um apartamento com banheiro para três dias, sim?
Sylvia	Sim.
Recepcionista	É o apartamento número quinze, no primeiro andar. Aqui tem a chave.
Sylvia	Muito obrigada.
Recepcionista	De nada.

boa tarde	*hello, good afternoon*
tem?	*do you have?*
apartamento (o)	*hotel room*
reservado	*reserved*
em meu nome	*in my name*
um momento	*just a second*
como se escreve?	*how do you write it?*
sobrenome (o)	*surname*
de	*of, from*
isso	*that's it*
com	*with*
banheiro (o)	*bathroom*
para	*for*
três	*three*
dias (os)	*days*
número (o)	*number*
quinze	*fifteen*
no primeiro andar	*on the first floor*
chave (a)	*key*
muito obrigada	*thanks very much*
de nada	*don't mention it*

Exercise 1

Tick **a** or **b** to complete the following statements.

1	Sylvia Peters is from	**a** London	**b** Manchester
2	She's going to stay	**a** 8 days	**b** 3 days
3	Her room no is	**a** 15	**b** 12

Grammar

A, an

The Portuguese words for *a (an)* are:

um (used with masculine words) **um apartamento** *a room*
uma (used with feminine words) **uma chave** *a key*

With more than one (i.e., in the plural), the words become:

uns (used with masculine plural words)
   uns apartamentos *some rooms*

umas (used with feminine plural words)
   umas chaves *some keys*

The

Similarly, Portuguese has four words to convey the English word *the*:

o *masculine singular* (i.e. one) **o apartamento** *the room*
a *feminine singular* **a chave** *the key*
os *masculine plural* **os apartamentos** *the rooms*
as *feminine plural* **as chaves** *the keys*

Plural nouns

When you have more than one item (noun), the basic way to form the plural is to add an -s, as in the examples above:

o apartamento   os apartamentos
a chave   as chaves

Beware of irregularities, which abound in Portuguese, such as **o mês** (*month*) **os meses** (*months*).

▶ Numbers

Here are the numbers 0 to 20, some of which have appeared in the first two dialogues.

0	zero	5	cinco
1	um, uma	6	seis
2	dois, duas	7	sete
3	três	8	oito
4	quatro	9	nove

10	dez	16	dezesseis
11	onze	17	dezessete
12	doze	18	dezoito
13	treze	19	dezenove
14	catorze (quatorze)	20	vinte
15	quinze		

Numbers *one* and *two* have both a masculine and a feminine form, so if you are talking about two houses, it's **duas** casas.

▶ Dialogue 3

Sylvia pops out in the evening to meet up with the Ferreiras. She knows José but has not yet met Mrs Ferreira.

José	Boa noite, Sylvia, tudo bem?
Sylvia	Oi, José, tudo bem.
José	Sylvia, esta é minha mulher Marli.
Sylvia	Muito prazer.
Marli	Igualmente. Bem-vinda a São Paulo. Como está?
Sylvia	Bem, obrigada.
José	Bom, vamos sentar? Que vão tomar?

boa noite	*hello, good evening/night*
tudo bem(?)	*everything OK(?)*
oi	*Hi*
esta (f)	*this*
minha mulher	*my wife*
muito prazer	*pleased to meet you*
igualmente	*likewise*
bem-vinda a São Paulo	*welcome to São Paulo*
bom	*right then*
vamos	*shall we/let's*
sentar	*to sit down*
que vão tomar?	*what are you going to have to drink?*

Exercise 2

Can you fill in the missing words from these statements?

a   _____ noite. Tudo _____?
b   Esta _____ minha mulher.
c   _____ prazer.

Grammar

This, these

When identifying people, or things, or when pointing them out, the words for *this* (*these*) are:

este (masculine person/thing) *this*   **esta** (feminine person/thing) *this*
estes (masculine plural)   *these* **estas** (feminine plural) *these*

este apartamento   *this room*   **estes apartamentos**   *these rooms*
esta chave *this key*   **estas chaves**   *these keys*

Possession: my, your, etc.

In the dialogues you were introduced to some of the possessive words: **seu** *your*, **minha** *my*. Here is the full table for *my* and *your*:

| | Singular | | Plural | |
	masculine	feminine	masculine	feminine
my	meu	minha	meus	minhas
your	seu	sua	seus	suas

The possessive word links to the item being possessed, and NOT the person to whom it belongs; therefore to say *my key*, you need to know that key is a feminine word; then choose **minha** from the table; **minha chave** = *my key*. Similarly, to say *your rooms*, you need to know that room is a masculine word, and it is in the plural, hence **seus apartamentos**. You will learn more possessives as you progress. Note that sometimes you will hear (or see) the possessive forms as, for example: **A sua chave; OS seus apartamentos**; with the appropriate word for *the* going with the possessed item.

(O) meu passaporte *my passport*   **(AS) suas chaves** *your keys*

Questions, questions

To ask basic questions in Portuguese, all you have to do is raise your voice in a questioning tone at the end of a statement: **Tudo bem**, *OK*. **Tudo bem?** *OK?*

You can also 'tag' question-phrases on to statements, e.g. **Você é inglesa, não é?** *You're English, aren't you?* **Um apartamento para três dias, sim?** *A room for three days, yes?* The answer to both of these questions is **Sim** *Yes*.

There are also question-words, known as interrogatives, with which you can begin a question. So far you have met:

Quanto? *How much?*   **Como?** *How?*   **Que?** *What?*

Summary

bom dia	*hello/good morning/goodbye*
boa tarde	*hello/good afternoon/goodbye*
boa noite	*hello/good evening/goodnight*
oi	*hi/hello*
tudo bem?	*how are things?/everything OK?*
como está?	*how are you?*
tudo bem	*fine/OK*
bem obrigado/a	*well, thanks*
tchau	*see you/bye*
muito prazer	*pleased to meet you*

i Greeting people

Brazilians are very tactile, open, friendly people, and it is common for them to kiss each other on greeting and saying goodbye. Men often shake hands with each other. Take your cue from their behaviour towards you and those around you.

i Brazilian police

Brazilian police at airports, border patrols, and in general, are not to be messed with! Make sure you have all your documentation in order (passport, visa, travel docs., driving licence, addresses of where you are staying). It is not unheard of for police to routinely check your vehicle and, inevitably, find something wrong with it. Often they are looking for a bribe, but you must be very careful here, as some travellers proffering money inside their passport have then been fined for so doing! The best policy, in many cases, is to keep quiet and pay the fine.

Practice

1   Now see if you can do the following:

   a   say *good morning, good afternoon, good evening*
   b   say *thank you, goodbye* (casually)
   c   say who you are
   d   ask if there is a room reserved in your name
   e   say *Hi, how are things?*

2 Give your part of the dialogue at the airport.

Inspetor	Boa tarde. Seu passaporte por favor.
You	(say *here it is*)
Inspetor	Você é inglês/inglesa?
You	(say *yes I am*)
Inspetor	Vai passar quanto tempo aqui?
You	(say *eight days*)
Inspetor	Muito bem. Tchau.
You	(say *goodbye*)

3 Work out the answers to these sums and write them out in words in Portuguese.

a dois e (and) cinco   =
b oito e seis   =
c dezenove menos (minus) dois =
d um e dez   =
e vinte menos sete   =

4 ▶ Look at the Bingo card below, and listen for your numbers being called out on the tape. Cross off any you hear, then write out in words in Portuguese the two you are left with.

12	3	18
6	10	9

5 Look at the pictures and link them to what people are saying.

6 ▶ Listen to the dialogue in the hotel, and tick the appropriate answers to the questions.

   a   What is the man's name?   John Harris ☐   John Peters ☐

   b   Where is he from?   London ☐   Liverpool ☐

   c   How long is he staying?   6 months ☐   6 days ☐

   d   What is his room number? 12 ☐   2 ☐

Do you understand?

Look at the following hotel booking-in form, and answer the questions that follow.

HOTEL SÃO LUÍS	
NOME:	*Senhor T. Andrews*
LUGAR DE ORIGEM:	*Londres*
N° DE DIAS:	*Seis*
TIPO DE APT°:	*Com banheiro*
N° DE APT°:	*treze*

1   Is the guest male or female?

2   S/he is Italian. True or false?

3   S/he is staying six days. True or false?

4   What type of room has s/he got?

5   S/he is in room no. 12. True or false?

02

você é casada?

are you married?

In this unit you will learn
- how to talk about yourself and your family
- how to talk about your home town
- how to give your address and telephone number

▶ Dialogue 1

Sylvia and the Ferreiras are sitting in a cafe in São Paulo. They are getting to know each other a bit better. The waiter (o garçom) brings their order.

Garçom Vamos ver. Um chope para o senhor Ferreira, um cafezinho para a senhora Ferreira, e um vinho tinto para a senhora.

José Obrigado.

Marli Você é de Manchester, não é?

Sylvia Sim, sou.

Marli E como é a cidade de Manchester?

Sylvia Bem, é grande e muito movimentada.

Marli Sylvia, você é casada? Tem filhos?

Sylvia Sim, tenho dois, um filho e uma filha.

Marli Como eles se chamam?

Sylvia Meu filho se chama Robert. Ele tem dezesseis anos e é estudante. Minha filha se chama Clare, tem vinte e três anos e é casada.

Marli E seu marido? Qual é o nome dele?

Sylvia Meu marido se chama Tony e ele trabalha numa empresa internacional que fabrica produtos químicos. E você, Marli, trabalha?

Marli Sim, sou professora de português numa escola de línguas. E você?

Sylvia Eu também trabalho – para uma empresa interessante; sou advogada.

vamos ver	*let's see*
um chope	*draught lager*
cafezinho (o)	*espresso coffee*
vinho tinto (o)	*red wine*
como é ...?	*what's ... like?*
cidade (a)	*city/town*
grande	*large*
movimentado	*busy*
casada	*married*
filhos (os)	*children*
tenho	*I have*
filho (o)	*son*
filha (a)	*daughter*
como eles se chamam?	*what are they called?*
se chama	*is called*

ele/ela tem ... anos	*he/she is ... years old*
vinte e três	*23*
estudante (o/a)	*student*
marido	*husband*
qual é o nome (dele)?	*what is (his) name?*
trabalha	*work(s)*
numa empresa	*in a company*
que	*that, which*
fabrica	*makes/produces*
produtos químicos (os)	*chemicals*
professora (a)	*teacher*
português	*Portuguese*
numa escola	*in a school*
línguas (as)	*languages*
trabalho	*I work*
internacional	*international*
interessante	*interesting*
advogada (a)	*lawyer*

True or false?

Say if these statements are **verdadeiro** or **falso**.

V   F

a   Sylvia is having beer.
b   Sylvia has three children.
c   Sylvia's daughter is married.
d   Marli is a maths teacher.
e   Sylvia is a lawyer.

Grammar

Describing places and people

You met adjectives (describing words) briefly in the first unit. Now let's have a look at them in more detail. Generally speaking, adjectives in Portuguese, unlike in English, go *after* the thing or person they are describing, e.g. **uma empresa internacional** *an international company*. Of course this does not apply if you are talking about something introduced by the verb *to be* e.g. **Londres é grande** *London is big,* where the word order is the same as in English.

The important point to remember is that if you are describing something (or someone) that is feminine, or in the plural, you must make the adjective match it by changing its ending – this is known as 'agreement of the adjective and noun'. Many adjectives end in -o (the masculine standard), such as **movimentado**. Look how it changes: **movimentado, movimentada, movimentados, movimentadas**. So, a busy city is **uma cidade movimentada**, and two busy countries are **dois países movimentados**.

Be on the look-out for irregular-ending words. In the dialogue you had:

grande	grande	grandes	grandes
interessante	interessante	interessantes	interessantes
internacional	internacional	internacionais	internacionais

Here are some adjectives you may want to use to describe your town (*town* = **a cidade** = fem.).

You will meet more adjectives as you progress.

pequeno	*small*	**lindo/bonito**	*pretty*
barulhento	*noisy*	**industrial**	*industrial*
histórico	*historical*	**litoral**	*coastal*
sossegado	*quiet*	**sujo**	*dirty*
cultural	*cultural*	**agricultural**	*agricultural*

Ter To have

You have now met various parts of the verb **ter** *to have*. Here it is in full for you to learn:

(eu) tenho	*I have*	(nós) temos	*we have*
(tu) tens*	*you have*		
(ele/ela) tem	*he/she/it has*	(eles/elas) têm	*they have*
(você) tem	*you have*	(vocês) têm	*you have* (plural)

*As this form is used in only some parts of Brazil, henceforth we shall concentrate on just four verbal forms. You will hear some Brazilians use **tu** plus the verb for **você**. Whilst being grammatically incorrect, it is nevertheless a colloquially recognized usage in some areas.

Note that **Ter** is used when you talk about your age, and not the verb *To be*, e.g. *I am 15* = **Tenho 15 anos**.

What is/are your/their name/s?

There are different ways to express names in Portuguese. You can say:

Qual é (seu) nome? *What is (your) name?* Or **Como (você) se chama?** *What are (you) called?* Or even **Quem é (você)?** *Who are (you)/is?*

Answers may be: **(meu) nome é ...** *(my) name is ...* Or **(me/se) chamo/a ...** *(I) am/is called ...* Or **sou/é ...** *I am / s/he is ...*

In the dialogue you were introduced to:

Como eles se chamam? *What are they called?*, and **Qual é o nome dele?** *What is his name?* Both of these are dealt with in following sections.

Verbs – present tense

In Portuguese, the ending of the verb (the action word) changes according to whoever is carrying out the action (the verb's subject). It is vital to get straight at this point the fact that it does not matter if the person is male or female, but whether they are 1st person (*I*, *we*), 2nd (*you*) or 3rd (*he*, *she*, *it*, *they*). Many people become confused when first approaching these verb forms, as they have just managed to master the concept of the **o/a** endings for male and female nouns and adjectives. Although these endings also appear on some verbs, they are NOT related to gender. Let's take a verb that you met in the dialogue and see what changes happen to it when we want different people to carry out the action.

You had examples of the verb *to work*: **trabalho** – *I work* and **trabalha** – *he works/you work*.

In Portuguese there are three main groups of verbs, as well as a variety of irregular oddities. The main groups are: Group 1 ending in **ar** – the most common; Group 2 ending in **er**; Group 3 ending in **ir**. The last two are very similar in endings. With only a few exceptions, all these verbs are formed in the same way:

- First you take off the (**-ar**) ending and you are left with what is called the stem, e.g. **trabalhar** (*to work*) – **trabalh**.
- Then you add on to this stem the appropriate ending according to whoever is doing the action.

- For -ar verbs, the endings you require are as follows :

stem +	
-o	*I*
-a	*he, she, it, you*
-amos	*we*
-am	*they, you* (plural)

Here are a few examples:

falo   *I speak*   **gostamos**   *we like*

trabalha   *he/she works/you work*   **moram**   *they, you live*

The meanings are sometimes ambiguous, so to make sure you really know who is doing the action, you may need to use the words for *he* (**ele**), *she* (**ela**), or *they* (**eles, elas**).

More verbs!

Some verbs are not content with changing their endings, but also have a little word accompanying them: **Se**. This word here means *self* or *selves*, so the question **Como eles se chamam?** actually means *what do they call themselves?* These 'self' words are known as 'reflexive pronouns', and they make the verb into a reflexive verb.

The full set you need to know is:

me   *myself*   **nos**   *ourselves*

se   *his/her/yourself/itself*   **se**   *them/yourselves*

You will see that they are placed before the verb. If you were in Portugal or speaking with a Portuguese person, they would usually place them afterwards. If you learnt some Portuguese before starting this course you may discover that in Brazil many of the rules of grammar are much more flexible than in Portugal.

More possessives: 'his/her'

To say *his/her* (and the plural *their*), in Portuguese, you should say *the (thing) of him/her/them*, as in the dialogue: **Qual é o nome dele?** *What is his name?/What is the name of him?*

The full forms are:

o/a ... dele	*his*	o/a ... dela	*her*
os/as ... dele	*his* (pl.)	os/as ... dela	*her* (pl.)

o/a ... deles	*their*	o/a ... delas	*their*
os/as ... deles	*their*	os/as ... delas	*their*
e.g as chaves deles	*their keys*	o nome dela	*her name*

You will also hear **seu/s (sua/s)**, the same form as *your*, but as this can cause confusion, it's better to use the other forms unless the context is completely unambiguous.

Compare **seu nome** *his/her/your name* and **o nome dele** *his name*.

Numa In a

Numa is actually two words squashed together (or contracted) for ease of pronunciation. They are: **em** (*in/on*) + **uma** (*a, fem.*) – **Numa** (*in/on a*), e.g. **numa escola** = *in a school*.

You will also find **num** (**em + um**), **nuns** (**em + uns**) and **numas** (**em + umas**), e.g. **nuns apartamentos** *in some rooms*.

In some written Portuguese the two words appear separated (e.g. **em uma ...**) although in practice people run them together when speaking.

Ser + professions

To talk about your, or other people's professions, you use **ser** (*to be*) plus the name of the profession, e.g. **sou professora** *I am a teacher*.

Note that there is no equivalent here to the English word *a*.

Here is a check list of some professions you may need to use. If yours is not here, your dictionary or teacher should be able to help you.

professor/a	*teacher*	**médico/a**	*doctor*
engenheiro/a	*engineer*	**advogado/a**	*lawyer*
dentista	*dentist*	**recepcionista**	*receptionist*
motorista	*driver*	**gerente**	*manager*
estudante	*student*	**secretário/a**	*secretary*

The full set of forms for **ser** is:

eu sou	*I am*	nós somos	*we are*
ele/ela é	*s/he, it is*	eles/elas são	*they are*
você é	*you are*	vocês são	*you* (pl.) *are*

Languages, nationalities

So far you have met **inglesa** (*English woman*) and **português** (*Portuguese*). Words of nationality, used also to describe the place of origin of something, are adjectives, and the name of each language is the masculine singular form. Look at the following table for more examples. Portuguese does not use capital letters.

	Nationality				Language spoken
	masc. sing.	*fem. sing.*	*masc. pl.*	*fem. pl.*	
Brazilian	brasileiro	brasileira	brasileiros	brasileiras	português
Portuguese	português	portuguesa	portugueses	portuguesas	português
English	inglês	inglesa	ingleses	inglesas	inglês
American	americano	americana	americanos	americanas	inglês
Spanish	espanhol	espanhola	espanhois	espanholas	espanhol
Argentine	argentino	argentina	argentinos	argentinas	espanhol
Chilean	chileno	chilena	chilenos	chilenas	espanhol
French	francês	francesa	franceses	francesas	francês
German	alemão	alemã	alemães	alemãs	alemão
Greek	grego	grega	gregos	gregas	grego

▶ Dialogue 2

José wants to note down some of Sylvia's details so that they can maintain links in the future.

José Qual é seu endereço em Manchester Sylvia?

Sylvia Oitenta e cinco Manor, m-a-n-o-r Road, Manchester, Inglaterra.

José Tem telefone?

Sylvia Sim, o número é 0161 – 236 – 553218, e o número do fax é 0161 – 236 – 553222.

José Está bem. E tem telefone aqui no hotel?

Sylvia Sim, estou no hotel Felix, o número é 678990, e estou no apartamento 15.

endereço (o)	*address*	**telefone (o)**	*telephone*
oitenta e cinco	*eighty-five*	**no hotel**	*in the hotel*
Inglaterra	*England*	**estou**	*I am*

True or false?

Say if these statements are **verdadeiro** or **falso**.

V   F

a Sylvia lives at 83 Manor Rd.
b She has no phone.
c She is in the Felix Hotel.

Grammar

▶ More numbers

Unfortunately, you cannot escape numbers – they surround us in everyday situations – money, time, dates. Here is another set for you to try to start learning.

21	vinte e um/uma	50	cinqüenta
22	vinte e dois/duas	60	sessenta
23	vinte e três	70	setenta
24	vinte e quatro	80	oitenta
25	vinte e cinco	90	noventa
30	trinta	100	cem (cento)
31	trinta e um/uma	101	cento e um
40	quarenta		

The word **e** (*and*) is used to join the two lots of digits together. **Cem** is used for a round 100 and **cento** for 101 and beyond.

Estar To be

To say where you are temporarily, you must use **estar**, the verb *to be* that describes anything temporary, including location e.g. **Estou no hotel** *I am in the hotel.*

The full set of forms for this verb are:

eu estou	*I am*	**nós estamos**	*we are*
ele/ela está	*he/she/it is*	**eles/elas estão**	*they are*
você está	*you are*	**vocês estão**	*you* (pl.) *are*

No hotel In the hotel

No is another example of a contracted pair of words, in this case **em + o** (*the*). It means *in the*. You will also find **na = em + a, nos = em + os, nas = em + as** (**nas cidades** *in the towns*).

You will also discover that the word **de** (*of, from*) contracts in the same way: **do/da/dos/das** e.g. **A chave do hotel** *the key of the hotel* (the hotel's key).

Countries

Most countries in Portuguese also fall into either a masculine or feminine group. Here are some examples:

Masculine countries		Feminine countries	
o Brasil	*Brazil*	a Inglaterra	*England*
o Canadá	*Canada*	a França	*France*
o México	*Mexico*	a Alemanha	*Germany*
o Japão	*Japan*	a Argentina	*Argentina*
o Peru	*Peru*	a Itália	*Italy*
o Reino Unido	*the UK*	a China	*China*
os Estados Unidos	*the USA*	a Espanha	*Spain*

So, to say *I am from England* you would say: **sou da (de + a) Inglaterra**, using the contracted form of **da**.

i When out at a café, Brazilians love to drink their **cafezinho** *little coffee* (strong, dark espresso), or when it's hot the **chope** – cooled draught national lager, the most well known being **Antártica**. One of this company's ads for its lager used to have the slogan **estupidamente gelada** *stupidly chilled* – it certainly makes sense when the temperature rises!

When giving someone a telephone number, if there is a six in the number, the Brazilians often say **meia** (*half*), and not seis.

Summary

como é ...?	*what's ... like?*
como se chama/m ...?	*what is/are he/she/you/ they called?*
qual é o (seu) nome?	*what's (your) name?*
tem ... anos	*is ... years old*
qual é seu endereço?	*what's your address?*
o número do telefone/ fax é ...	*the telephone/ fax number is ...*

Practice

1 Complete your part of the dialogue. José is trying to find out more about you.

José Você é de Liverpool?
You (say *no, I'm from Birmingham*)
José Como é a cidade de Birmingham?
You (say *it's big and industrial*)
José Tem filhos?
You (say *yes, I have one son*)
José Qual é o nome dele?
You (say *he is called David. He is 28 years old and is a French teacher*)
José Você trabalha?
You (Say *yes, I work for an international company*)

2 Match up the telephone numbers in digits and Portuguese.

a quatro dois um cinco três três   **i** 368475
b seis seis oito quatro quatro zero   **ii** 553311
c três meia oito quatro sete cinco   **iii** 421533
d cinco cinco três três um um   **iv** 904621
e nove zero quatro meia dois um   **v** 668440

3 ▶ Listen to someone describing their family, work and town, and tick which pictures apply to the descriptions given.

1 a

b

2 a

b

3 a

b

4 a

b

4 Fill in the gaps with appropriate words for numbers/nouns/adjectives.

a Tenho (5) _____ chaves (*small*) _____.
b Sra Ferreira é _____ (*Brazilian*).
c Sylvia tem três _____ _____ (*interesting, children*).
d Sou de Paris; é uma cidade _____ (*historical*).
e Marli tem _____ _____ _____ (*2, German wines*).

Do you understand?

One of Marli's students has received a letter from a new penfriend. Can you read it and answer the questions on it?

Brasília, 8 de janeiro

Olá Maria,

Tudo bem? Eu estou muito bem. Vou te dizer um pouco sobre quem sou. Meu nome é Vania, tenho vinte e dois anos e sou de Brasília.

É uma cidade super-grande e moderna, e muito interessante. Não sou casada. Sou estudante de línguas e também trabalho numa escola secundária; sou secretária.

Tchau, Vania

> **vou te dizer um pouco sobre quem sou**   *I'm going to tell you a bit about who I am*

1 How old is Vania?
2 What is Brasília like?
3 Is she married?
4 What does she do?
5 Now write a short letter like this about yourself.

(You will find an example in the Key to the exercises, on p. 205).

03 onde é sua cidade?

where is your town?

In this unit you will learn

- how to describe where your home town is
- how to describe your belongings and recover lost property
- how to describe what things are made of
- about colours

▶ Dialogue 1

Sylvia goes to the Ferreiras' house to arrange her stay there. She chats to the daily help (a **faxineira**), Dona Rita.

Sylvia	Bom dia. Sou Sylvia Peters, amiga da senhora Ferreira.
D. Rita	Bom dia, senhora. Como está?
Sylvia	Bem, obrigada, e a senhora?
D. Rita	Eu estou bem, graças a Deus.
Sylvia	Marli está?
D. Rita	Ela já vem da escola. A senhora não é daqui, é?
Sylvia	Não, sou inglesa. Sou de Manchester.
D. Rita	E como é a sua cidade? É uma cidade grande como aqui? Onde é? Perto de Londres?
Sylvia	Bom, Manchester é uma cidade interessante e bastante grande, mas não como São Paulo.
D. Rita	E sua família mora lá com você?
Sylvia	Mora, sim, mas também tenho família no centro da Inglaterra, em Birmingham, e também numa cidade pequena ao sul do país, perto de Londres. Manchester não é perto de Londres, mas ao noroeste do país.
D. Rita	Aqui está a senhora Ferreira. Vão pegar suas malas, não é?
Sylvia	Sim, vamos para o hotel agora e voltamos para o jantar.

amiga (a)	*friend*	**com**	*with*
estou bem	*I'm well*	**no centro de**	*in the centre of*
graças a Deus	*thank goodness*	**ao sul de**	*to the south of*
Marli está?	*is Marli at home?*	**país (o)**	*country*
ela já vem	*she's on her way*	**perto de**	*near to*
daqui	*from here*	**pegar**	*to get/fetch*
como aqui	*like here*	**malas (as)**	*suitcases*
bastante grande	*quite big*	**vamos**	*we're going*
não como ...	*not like ...*	**agora**	*now*
mora	*live*	**voltamos**	*we'll return*
lá	*there*	**jantar (o)**	*dinner*
onde é	*where is?*		

True or false?

Tick **verdadeiro** or **falso** for the following statements based on the dialogue.

V F

a   Marli está em casa (*at home*).
b   Sylvia tem família em Manchester.

c   Londres é longe de Manchester.
d   Marli e Sylvia vão para o hotel.
e   Elas vão jantar no hotel.

Grammar

X's friend

When talking about possession in the 3rd person (he/she/it/they), remember you learnt to say *the (thing) of him/her*, etc. in Unit 2. The same applies if you want to use alternatives to him/her, such as *the teacher's key, the student's room*, etc. You must turn the sentence around in Portuguese and say:

the key of the teacher – **a chave do professor (da professora)**
the room of the students – **o apartamento dos estudantes.**

In the dialogue you met '**amiga da senhora Ferreira**' – *Mrs Ferreira's friend.*

'Mr' and 'Mrs'

The expressions for *Mr* and *Mrs* are (**o**) **senhor** (**sr**) and (**a**) **senhora** (**sra**). These combine with words such as **de** to form **do sr/da sra**, e.g. **a casa do senhor Villas Boas** *Mr Villas Boas' house.*

Locations

If you are describing where your home town or place of work is, the following may be useful:

no/*ao norte (de)	*in/to the north (of)*	**no/ao leste**	*in the east*
no/ao sul	*in the south*	**no/ao oeste**	*in the west*
ao/no centro (de)	*in the centre (of)*	**na costa**	*on the coast*
no interior	*inland*	**no litoral**	*on the coast*
perto de	*near*	**longe de**	*far (from)*

***ao** = **a** (*to/at*) + **o** (*the*). Other contractions involving the word **a** (which is known as a preposition – a locating word) are:

a + a = à
a + os = aos   cásas
a + as = às

Try not to be thrown off balance by the fact that the word **a** in Portuguese also means *the* in the feminine form.

Liverpool é ao norte da Inglaterra.	*Liverpool is in the north of England.*
Brasília é no centro do Brasil.	*Brasília is in the centre of Brazil.*
Campinas é no interior de São Paulo.	*Campinas is in the interior of São Paulo (State).*

Ir To go

You met parts of this important irregular verb in the dialogue: **vão** – *you (pl.) are going*, and **vamos** – *we're going* (also meaning *let's ...*).

In full, the verb is:

vou	*I'm going/I go*	**vamos**	*we're going/go*
vai	*s/he's going/s/he goes*	**vão**	*they're going/they go*
	you're going/you go		*you're going/you go* (pl.)
	it's going/it goes		

▶ Dialogue 2

Sylvia realizes she left her bag in the taxi on the way to the Ferreiras'. Marli takes her to the taxi lost property office (**a seção de perdidos e achados**) where she talks to an employee (**empregado**).

Empregado	Bom, vamos ver. Uma bolsa, sim?
Sylvia	Isso. É bem pequena.
Empregado	E de que é? De couro, de plástico, de quê?
Sylvia	De couro.
Empregado	E de que cor é?
Sylvia	Preta e roxa. *Black $\wp$ White Purple*
Empregado	E tem alguma coisa dentro?
Sylvia	Sim, tem a chave do hotel, uma carteira com dinheiro, minha agenda, e meus óculos de sol amarelos.
Empregado	É esta? (*shows her a bag*)
Sylvia	Sim, é. Obrigada. É muito gentil.
Empregado	De nada. Faça o favor de assinar aqui. Bom dia.

bolsa (a)	bag	carteira (a)	purse/wallet
de que é	what's it	dinheiro (o)	money
	(made) of?	agenda (a)	diary
(de) couro	leather	óculos de	
(de) plástico	plastic	sol (os)	sunglasses
de que cor é?	what colour is it?	amarelos	yellow
preto	black	gentil	kind
roxo	purple	faça o favor	
alguma coisa	something	de assinar	please sign
dentro	inside		

Exercise

Answer **sim** *yes* or **não** *no* to these statements.

a   A bolsa de Sylvia é de couro.   *Sim*

b   É preta.   *Sim*

c   Tem o passaporte dentro.   *Não*

Grammar

De que é (feito)? What's it made of?

To describe what something is made from, Portuguese often uses
the structure: a (thing) of (material). Look at these examples:

De:	**plástico**	*plastic*	**papel**	*paper*
	couro	*leather*	**lã**	*wool*
	vidro	*glass*	**algodão**	*cotton*
	metal	*metal*	**pedra**	*stone*
	madeira	*wood*	**tijolo**	*brick/tile*

e.g. **uma bolsa de plástico** *a plastic bag*, **uma toalha de
algodão** *a cotton towel*. You can of course find examples such
as **uma bolsa plástica** and **uma chave metálica**.

Colours

You will also need to know **as cores** *colours* to describe personal
possessions, or even features of people (eyes, etc.).

Remember that **as cores** *colours* are adjectives. They must
change their endings where appropriate to match the noun(s)
they are describing. They also go after the noun, e.g.

preto	black	verde	green
branco	white	marrom	
roxo	purple	(pl. = marrons)	brown
azul		vermelho	red
(pl. = azuis)	blue	laranja	orange
amarelo	yellow	rosa	pink
escuro	dark	claro	light

uma chave branca	*a white key*
dois passaportes azuis	*two blue passports*
óculos marrons escuros	*dark brown glasses*

'Please'

One of the polite ways of asking people to do things is by using the structure of **faça o favor de + verb**. This is literally *do the favour of ... ing*. You can use it with any verb. To ask more than one person to do something, change **faça** to **façam**. For example, **Façam o favor de trabalhar** *Please work*.

You may also hear another form, **faz o favor de ...**, with an identical meaning when talking to just one person.

Ser/Estar – an overview

You learnt the formation for these two verbs in the last unit. Let's look more closely at when you should use each one.

ser

Professions	Sou professora
Nationality	É inglesa?
Permanent location	É no centro
Permanent characteristics	É grande/preto
Place of origin	Sou de ...

estar

Temporary location	Aqui está
Temporary condition	Como está?
Position	Está dentro

Bags and briefcases

Here are some suggestions for vocabulary you may need when describing the contents of your bag.

o passaporte	*passport*
o telefone portátil (o telemóvel)	*mobile phone*
uma caneta	*pen*
um lenço	*handkerchief*
os comprimidos	*tablets*
o livro de endereços	*address book*
os bilhetes de ...	*tickets for ...*
um pente	*comb*
o batom	*lipstick*
o isqueiro	*cigarette lighter*

Summary

como é sua cidade?	*what's your town like?*
onde é (sua cidade?)	*where is it (your town)?*
... é uma cidade ...	*... is a ... town*
é grande/interessante/pequena	*it's big/interesting/small*
ao norte/sul/leste/oeste	*to/in the north/south/east/west*
faça/m o favor de ...	*please ...*
de que é feito?	*what's it made of?*
é de couro/vidro/lã	*it's made of leather/ glass/wool*
de que cor é?	*what colour is it?*
é preto/azul/vermelho	*it's black/blue/red*

Practice

1 Decide which verb *to be* (**ser/estar**) you should use in each example, and write the correct form of it.

a José _____ do Brasil.

b As cidades _____ grandes.

c Minha chave _____ dentro da bolsa.

d João tem um filho; ele _____ médico.

e _____ Ángela, _____ americana.

2 Fill in your part of the dialogue, about where you're from.

Sônia	Você é de Nova Iorque, não é?
You	(say *no, I'm from Brighton*)
Sônia	Onde é Brighton?
You	(say *it's a small town in the south of England*)
Sônia	É perto de Londres?
You	(say *yes, it's quite near*)

3 ▶ Listen to someone describing their bag and its contents. Tick the relevant pictures below, according to what you hear.

4 ▶ Look at the map below and listen to the description of where certain towns are located. See if you can correctly mark where the towns should be.

São Paulo state

São Paulo capital

1 =
2 =
3 =
4 =
5 =

Choose from:

Santos   Uberaba

Piracicaba

Campinas   Catanduva

Do you understand?

Look at the following postcard, and say if the statements below are **verdadeiro** or **falso**.

oi Paulo,

Estou num hotel no centro da Inglaterra. A cidade é pequena, mas é perto de Birmingham que é grande e interessante.

Um beijo da ··· Ana

Paulo R. da Silva
R. Mem Martin, 25
Piracicaba-SP
10325
Brasil

V   F

1 Ana is staying with relatives.
2 She is in the Northwest of England.
3 The town is not far from Birmingham.
4 She thinks Birmingham is boring.

04

há uma farmácia por aqui?

is there a chemist's around here?

In this unit you will learn

- how to ask for and understand basic directions
- how to talk about the weather
- how to understand time
- how to say *there is/there are*

▶ Dialogue 1

Sylvia pops into the city centre (**o centro**). First of all she needs a chemist.

Sylvia	Desculpe. Há uma farmácia por aqui?
Transeunte	(*passer-by*) Aqui, nesta rua não há, mas há uma na Rua Cabral.
Sylvia	E onde é esta rua?
Transeunte	Bem, você vai por aqui em frente, vira à esquerda naquela esquina, depois você segue em frente mais um pouco, toma a segunda à direita, e a farmácia é aí.
Sylvia	Fica muito longe?
Transeunte	Não, é só dez minutos.
Sylvia	Obrigada.

desculpe	*excuse me*
há	*there is/are; is/are there?*
farmácia (a)	*chemist's*
por aqui	*round here*
nesta rua não há	*there isn't one in this street*
mas	*but*
você: vai/vira/segue/toma	*you/go/turn/follow/take*
em frente	*in front/ahead*
à esquerda/direita	*on the left/right*
mais um pouco	*a little more*
a segunda	*the second*
é aí	*it's there*
fica muito longe?	*is it a long way off?*
é só dez minutos	*it's only ten minutes*
naquela esquina	*on that street corner*

Exercise 1

Can you answer the following questions based on the dialogue?

                                                   Yes   **No**

a Is there a chemist's where Sylvia is?

b Does Sylvia have to turn left?

c Is the chemist's a long way off?

Grammar

Is there ...?

To ask if there is a particular shop near where you are, you say **há** (*is/are there*) [a shop] **por aqui?** You can also talk about such locations as: **aqui perto/perto daqui** – *near (to) here*, **nesta rua/cidade** – *in this street/town*. If you are lucky, the answer will be: **sim, há.** In the dialogue the answer was negative (**não há**), but at least the passer-by helpfully explained where the nearest chemist's was. You can also use **tem...?** as an alternative to **há.**

To be more specific in your request for information, use: **onde é?** – *where is?* or **onde há** – *where is there (a)?* Understanding the directions is another matter!

Directions

To begin with you need to know your basic directions:

à esquerda <	em frente ^	à direita >
left	*straight on*	*right*

Then, some basic instructions:

você vai	*you go*
vira	*turn*
segue	*carry on*
toma	*take*

And you will finally discover what you're looking for:

e ... é aí/fica aí/é por aí – *and ... is there/over there*

You may want to check: **fica longe/perto?** – *is it a long way/near?* or **é longe daqui?** – *is it a long way from here?* If you're lucky the answer will be: **é perto!**

You may well make use of expressions such as:

Pode repetir por favor? *Can you repeat that please?* **Não compreendo muito bem** *I don't understand very well.* **Fale mais devagar** *Speak more slowly.*

Nesta, naquela In this, in that

These are two more examples of contracted words. **Nesta** comes from **em + esta** (*this*) (you met the other forms of **esta** in Unit 1). **Naquela** comes from **em + aquela** (*that*). The full forms of *that/those* are:

aquele (m.)	aquela (f.)	aqueles (m. pl.)	aquelas (f. pl.)
aquele senhor	*that man*	aquelas ruas	*those streets*
naquela rua	*in that street*	naqueles livros	*in those books*

▶ First to fifth

When requesting directions, you also need to know some ordinal numbers, so that you can turn down the appropriate street. Here are a few to get you going. You will need more of them if you are visiting people who live on the 20th floors of high-rise blocks!

1st	primeiro	*2nd*	segundo	*3rd*	terceiro
4th	quarto	*5th*	quinto		

These are adjectives and as such will change their endings to agree with the noun they are describing, e.g. *the second key* = **a segunda chave**, *the 4th street* = **a quarta rua**.

▶ Dialogue 2

Sylvia now needs to find a bank.

Sylvia   Desculpe. Sabe se há um banco perto daqui?
Transeunte   Sim, há um banco no fim da rua, à direita.
Sylvia   E sabe se está aberto agora?
Transeunte   Que horas são?
Sylvia   São onze e meia.
Transeunte   Então, sim, está aberto. Aqui os bancos abrem das oito e meia da manhã até às três horas da tarde.

sabe se	*do you know if*
no fim da rua	*at the end of the street*
está aberto	*is open*
que horas são?	*what time is it?*
são onze e meia	*it's 11.30*
então	*well then*
os bancos abrem	*the banks open*
das 8 e meia da manhã	*from 8.30 in the morning*
até às 3 horas da tarde	*until 3 pm*

True or false?

Say whether the following are **verdadeiro** (**V**) or **falso** (**F**).

a   Há um banco perto.
b   O banco não está aberto.
c   Os bancos abrem até às 4 horas da tarde.

Grammar

Spend, spend, spend!!!

Here is a check-list of some of the shops and establishments you may need to talk about.

as lojas	*shops*	**o correio**	*post office*
o mercado	*market*	**a farmácia**	*chemist's*
o supermercado	*supermarket*	**o turismo**	*tourist*
o hotel	*hotel*		*information*
o restaurante	*restaurant*	**a loja**	
o café	*café*	**de roupas**	*clothes shop*
o banco	*bank*	**o açougue**	*butcher's*

You will find more on shops in Unit 7.

Time

To ask the time you say **Que horas são?** – literally *what hours are they?* Answers will be:

São duas horas. São três horas. São quatro horas. São cinco horas.

São seis horas. São sete horas. São oito horas. São nove horas.

São dez horas.   São onze horas.   São doze horas.

É meio-dia/meia-noite/uma hora – *It's midday/midnight/one o'clock*

Time past the hour is expressed as:

X (horas) e Y (minutos), e.g. **São cinco e vinte** *It's twenty past five*. Quarter and half past are: **X e um quarto/X e meia**.

Time to the hour is expressed as minutes to (**para**) the next hour, e.g. **São dez para as oito** = *it's ten to eight*.

Opening and closing times: **aberto/a** = *open* and **fechado/a** = *closed*.

People will express shop times as follows: ... **abre/fecha (está aberto/fechado) das ... (horas) até às ... horas** e.g. **O turismo abre das nove e um quarto até às dez para as cinco** = *The tourist office opens from 9.15 till 4.50.*

This can be qualified with the part of the day in question: **da manhã/da tarde/da noite** – *in the morning/in the afternoon/at night*, e.g. **até às três horas da tarde** = *until three in the afternoon*.

Dialogue 3

Sylvia stops at the **quiosque** in the square to buy a newspaper (**um jornal**).

Sylvia	Boa tarde. Uma Folha de São Paulo por favor.
Vendedora	São 2 reais.
Sylvia	Que calor, não é?
Vendedora	Pois é, hoje está muito quente. A senhora não é daqui, é?
Sylvia	Não, sou inglesa.
Vendedora	Ah, na Inglaterra sempre chove, não é?
Sylvia	Chove muito, mas no verão também faz calor. Mas aqui na cidade não venta, e está muito abafado.
Vendedora	É sempre assim – ainda pior por causa da poluição aqui. Eu nao agüento estes dias.
Sylvia	Nem eu. Bom, tenho de ir. Tchau.

Folha de São Paulo	*São Paulo daily paper*
por favor	*please*
que calor	*isn't it hot*
são ... reais	*that's ... reais*
hoje	*today*
quente	*hot*
sempre	*always*
chove	*it rains*
no verão	*in the summer*
faz calor	*it's hot*
abafado	*stifling/close*
é sempre assim	*it's always like this*
ainda pior	*even worse*
por causa de	*because of*
poluição (a)	*pollution*
não agüento	*I can't stand*
nem eu	*me neither*
tenho de ir	*I have to go*

Exercise 2

See if you have understood the dialogue. Choose the correct answers from the boxes.

1 How much is the paper? **a** 2 reais   **b** 3 reais
2 The vendor thinks in England it's always **a** raining **b** windy
3 One of the contributing factors to the heavy atmosphere is
    a pollution   **b** clouds

Grammar

The weather

There are various ways to describe **o tempo** *the weather*:

Verb		Expressions			
fazer	*to do/make*	**faz calor**	*it's hot*	**faz frio**	*it's cold*
estar	*to be*	**está quente**	*it's hot*	**está frio**	*it's cold*
		está abafado	*it's close*		
chover	*to rain*			**chove**	*it rains*
nevar	*to snow*			**neva**	*it snows*

Ser is only used with weather expressions if you are describing a permanent state, such as climate: **É sempre frio no inverno no Canadá** – *It's always cold in winter in Canada.*

i Most shops in Brazil open from 8.30 to 6.30. On Saturdays they open until lunchtime, and it is rare to find anything except cafés or large shopping centres open on Sundays.

The summer months can become quite intolerable heat-wise, especially if you are away from the coast. Remember the seasons in Brazil are the opposite to the northern hemisphere. The hottest time is January – March.

Brazilian currency is the **real** (pl. **reais**). Inflation in Brazil is notorious for its eccentricity, running over 100% and more, although in recent years it has shown signs of steadying.

Some Brazilian publications are available outside the country and make good reading practice. You could try getting hold of **Folha de São Paulo**, or **Veja** (like *Time*).

Summary

há/tem um/a ... por aqui?	*is there a ... round here?*
à esquerda/direita	*on the left/right*
fica (muito) longe/perto?	*is it (very) far/near?*
está aberto/fechado?	*is it open/closed?*
são ... horas	*it's ... o'clock*
abrem das ... até às ...	*they open from ... to ...*
da manhã/tarde/noite	*in the morning/afternoon/ evening*
por favor	*please*
está quente/frio	*it's hot/cold*

Practice

1   Can you do the following?

    a   ask if there is a butcher's near here
    b   ask where there is a post office
    c   ask what time it is
    d   say *it's 2.30pm*
    e   say *in Germany it rains a little*

2 Look at the clocks below and match them to the times given.

i são cinco e meia **ii** é meio-dia/meia noite **iii** são vinte e cinco
para as nove **iv** são três e um quarto **v** é um quarto para as dez

3 Look at the map on page 50, then read the directions. In each case say where you would end up if you correctly followed the instructions.

Instructions: starting outside your hotel (* on map).

a Vira à esquerda, toma a segunda rua à direita, e vai em frente. _____ fica na esquina.

b Vai em frente, e _____ é ali à direita. É muito perto.

c Vira à esquerda, segue em frente um pouco, depois toma a primeira à esquerda, e _____ é ali em frente.

d Vai em frente, e segue a rua um pouco. Toma a segunda à esquerda, depois vira à esquerda, e toma a primeira à direita. _____ é aí em frente.

4 ▶ Listen to someone describing the weather today in various countries (England, Brazil, France, Mexico, Japan) and link up the weather pictures with the appropriate country.

5 Fill in your part of this dialogue. You are trying to find out about the local market.

You   (Say *excuse me do you know if there is a market near here*)

Transeunte   Sim, há um no fim da rua.

You   (Say *do you know if it is open now*)

Transeunte   Que horas são?

You   (Say *it's 10.15*)

Transeunte   Então, sim, está aberto.

You   (Ask *is it far?*)

Transeunte   Não, é só cinco minutos.

You   (Say *thanks and goodbye*)

6 Fill in the gaps below with words from the box.

a Onde _____ o mercado?

b É _____ em frente.

c _____ são meus filhos.

d Toma a _____ rua à esquerda.

e São dez _____ as oito.

> aqueles   terceira   fica   para   ali

Do you understand?

Read this message that has been left for Sylvia, and answer the questions below.

Sylvia

Pode fazer um favor para mim, e ir ao correio com as cartas?

Vai daqui à esquerda, vira à direita na rua Gomes Sá, e toma a segunda à esquerda que é a rua Nascimento. O correio fica ali em frente. Abre das nove e quinze até às quatro da tarde.

Não é muito longe!

Obrigada

Marli.

1 Where does Marli want Sylvia to go?
2 Where should she turn right?
3 Which street on the left should she take?
4 What time does the place close?
5 Is it very far?

05 a que horas começa?

what time do you start?

In this unit you will learn
- how to discuss your work
- how to discuss how you travel to work
- how to talk about daily routines

▶ Dialogue 1

Sylvia and the Ferreiras have gone on a trip to Santos, the most important port on the southern Brazilian coast.

Sylvia Meu Deus! É tão grande – e movimentado. Quantas pessoas trabalham aqui?

José Não sei exatamente, mas deve ser um número enorme. É o porto mais importante do Brasil.

Marli É mais importante do que Liverpool. Você vê todos os barcos ali? Vêm de toda parte do mundo.

Sylvia Incrível. Marli, me diga uma coisa – a escola onde você trabalha – tem quantos alunos?

Marli Tem mais ou menos cento e vinte alunos – dos catorze aos vinte e cinco anos.

Sylvia Então, é uma escola bastante grande. Você come lá durante o dia?

Marli Não, a escola não tem refeitório mas eu almoço num café bem perto.

Sylvia A que horas começa?

Marli Começo às oito e um quarto, tenho uma hora e meia para o almoço, e saio às seis da tarde. Às vezes tenho uma turma à noite.

Sylvia Tanto trabalho!

Marli É mesmo!

meu Deus!	*my God/goodness me*
tão	*so*
quantas pessoas	*how many people*
não sei exatamente	*I don't know exactly*
deve ser	*it must be*
enorme	*enormous*
porto (o)	*port*
mais importante do/do que	*most important in the/than*
você vê?	*can you see?*
todos	*all*
barcos (os)	*boats*
vêm	*come*
toda parte	*every part*
mundo (o)	*world*
incrível	*incredible*
diga uma coisa	*tell me*
alunos (os)	*pupils*
mais ou menos	*more or less*

come	you eat
durante	during
refeitório (o)	canteen
almoço/almoço (o)	I lunch/lunch
bem perto	really near
a que horas	at what time
começa/começo	you/I begin
saio	I leave/go out
às vezes	sometimes
turma (a)	class/group
tanto trabalho	so much work
é mesmo	you're right

Exercise 1

Choose the correct words to fill in the gaps.

a Santos é um porto muito _____ grande/pequeno.
b Marli come o almoço _____ num restaurante/num café.
c Marli trabalha _____ muito/pouco.

Grammar

O mais importante The most important

When making comparisons between two things, places or people, Portuguese uses **mais de** *more* or **menos de** *less*. The structure is: **X é mais (menos)** *ADJECTIVE* **do que Y**. For example:

Santos é mais importante do que Liverpool.

Often in spoken Portuguese, the **do que** becomes just **que**. The superlative (i.e. the highest degree) of these comparisons is expressed as: **X é o/a _____ mais** *ADJECTIVE*. For example:

Santos é o (porto) mais importante.

Some adjectives have slightly irregular forms of comparison. Look at the table below.

Adjective	Comparative	Superlative
alto *tall*	**mais alto** *taller*	**o mais alto** *the tallest*
grande *big*	**maior** *bigger*	**o maior** *the biggest*
pequeno *small*	**menor** *smaller*	**o menor** *the smallest*
bom *good*	**melhor** *better*	**o melhor** *the best*
mau *bad*	**pior** *worse*	**o pior** *the worst*

Study these examples:

José é mais alto do que Marli.	*José is taller than Marli.*
O tempo hoje está melhor.	*The weather today is better.*
Ela é a pior aluna.	*She is the worst pupil.*

More verbs

In Unit 2 you learnt how to use all the parts of the **-ar** verb **trabalhar**. To talk about daily routines you need to know how to form verbs from the other two main groups.

	-er comer *to eat*	-ir partir *to leave*
eu	com*o*	part*o*
ele/ela	com*e*	part*e*
você	com*e*	part*e*
nós	com*emos*	part*imos*
eles/elas	com*em*	part*em*
vocês	com*em*	part*em*

You will see that the endings for these two groups are very similar.

Ver, vir To see, to come

Irregular verbs are always awkward, and you must concentrate hard in order to learn them adequately. Two verbs most commonly mixed up are **ver** and **vir**. Look at the two of them in the present tense.

ver *to see*	vir *to come*
vejo	venho
vê	vem
vemos	vimos
vêem	vêm

Todo, todas All, every

Todo is an adjective meaning *all/every*, and has four parts agreeing with what it is describing.

todo	toda	todos	todas

You will also come across **tudo**. This is a neuter word meaning *everything/all that*, which is non-specific. It never changes form.

todo (o) dia/todos os dias	*every day*
todas as pessoas	*all the people/everyone*
tudo é bom	*everything is good*

The numbers game 100–1000

Here are some more numbers for you to learn.

101	cento e um, uma	150	cento e cinqüenta
102	cento e dois, duas	160	cento e sessenta
105	cento e cinco	170	cento e setenta
110	cento e dez	180	cento e oitenta
120	cento e vinte	190	cento e noventa
130	cento e trinta	199	cento e noventa e nove
140	cento e quarenta		

▶ These are on the recording.

100	cem	600	seiscentos/as
200	duzentos/as	700	setecentos/as
300	trezentos/as	800	oitocentos/as
400	quatrocentos/as	900	novecentos/as
500	quinhentos/as	1.000	mil

Use the feminine form of these numbers if you are discussing feminine items, e.g. **trezentas milhas** (*300 miles*). Hundreds, tens and units are each divided by **e**. After thousands there is no **e**, except if the thousand if followed by 1–100, or when followed by 200–999 if the last two numbers are zeros.

Time

Saying at what time things happen is not much different from what you learnt in the previous unit.

às ... (horas)	*at ... (o' clock)*
às ... e ...	*at ...*
às ... para ...	*at ... to ...*
à uma hora	*at one o' clock*
ao meio dia/à meia-noite	*at midday/midnight*

Look at these examples:

às cinco horas	*at five o' clock*
às dez e vinte	*at 10.20*
às quinze para as oito	*at 7.45*

Dialogue 2

José asks Sylvia about her daily routine.

José   Sylvia, você mora mesmo em Manchester?

Sylvia   Bem, moro a cinco quilômetros de Manchester, numa pequena aldeia, mas trabalho em Manchester.

José   Como é que você vai ao trabalho? Vai de carro?

Sylvia   Não, de manhã e à tarde o trânsito é impossível, por isso vou de bicicleta no verão. Saio de casa às oito e chego ao trabalho às oito e meia.

José   E no inverno – também vai de bicicleta no frio?

Sylvia   Não, não tenho coragem – em Manchester chove muito no inverno. Ou vou de ônibus, ou pego uma carona com uma amiga.

José   A que horas sai do escritório à tarde?

Sylvia   Em geral saio de lá por volta das cinco e meia, mas às vezes fico trabalhando até às seis, seis e um pouco.

mesmo em Manchester	*in Manchester itself*
a 5 quilômetros de	*5 km from*
aldeia(a)	*village*
como vai a …?	*how do you get to …?*
de carro/bicicleta/ônibus	*by car/bike/bus*
trânsito (o)	*traffic*
impossível	*impossible*
por isso	*for that reason/so*
verão (o)	*summer*
chego	*I arrive*
inverno (o)	*winter*
coragem (a)	*courage*
ou … ou …	*either … or …*
pego uma carona	*I get a lift*
amiga (a)	*friend*
escritório (o)	*office*
em geral	*generally*
por volta de	*around*
às vezes	*sometimes*
fico trabalhando	*I stay working*

Exercise 2

Say if these statements are **verdadeiro** or **falso**.

V   F

a   Sylvia lives in Manchester itself.
b   In summer she cycles to work.
c   Sometimes she works until 9 pm.

Grammar

... é que ...? ... is it that ...?

Often, the expression **é que** (*is it that*) is inserted into a question to either emphasize something important, or simply to enhance the flow of the sentence. If you have studied French, you will recognize the expression *est-ce que*.

Transport

To talk about means of transport, you use a verb (usually **ir** – *to go*), plus **de** plus the transport. There are a couple of exceptions. The following table contains some examples.

de	**carro** *car* **ônibus** *bus* **bicicleta** *bicycle* **ônibus (de luxo)** *coach* **metrô** *underground* **motocicleta** *motorbike* **aviāo** *aeroplane* **trem** *train* **barco** *boat*	**a**	**cavalo** *horse* **pé** *foot*

Two irregular verbs – pedir/sair

These two verbs have certain irregularities, so be careful when using them. In the present tense they are:

pedir *to ask for*	**sair** *to go out*
peço	saio
pede	sai
pedimos	saimos
pedem	saem

Summary

é o/a mais ... de ...	*it's the most ... in the ...*
é mais/menos ... (de) que ...	*it's more/less ... than ...*
a que horas começa/termina?	*at what time do you start/ finish?*
começo/termino às ...	*I start/finish at ...*
ao meio dia/à meia noite	*at midday/midnight*
(você) mora em ...?	*do you live in ...?*
como vai ao trabalho?	*how do you get to work?*
vou de carro/bicicleta/táxi	*I go by car/bicycle/taxi*
saio por volta das ...	*I leave about ... o'clock*
fico trabalhando até ...	*I stay/remain working until ...*

Practice

1 ▶ Look at the following extract from Nelson's diary, then listen to him describing his daily routine and fill in the gaps in his diary with activities or times, as though he has written it himself.

8.15	a ?
8.50	*chego ao trabalho*
9.00	b ?
10.00	
c ?	*como o almoço*
d ?	
17.35	
e ?	*chego em casa*

2 Fill in the gaps with appropriate times.

a Sónia sai de casa _____   a

b Miguel vai ao trabalho _____   b

c   Ana pega o ônibus _____   c

d   Eu saio da escola _____   d

e   José come o almoço _____   e

f   Sylvia chega em casa _____   f

3 Make sentences describing where places are in relation to each other, writing out in Portuguese the distances.
   a [Portugal] é a [600 km] da [France].
   b [Brazil] é a [1896 km] do [Mexico].
   c [England] é a [1247 km] de [Portugal].
   d [USA] são a [6,125 km] da [Argentina].

4 Match the questions with the answers.
   a Como vai ao trabalho?   i   Mais ou menos 120.
   b Quantas pessoas trabalham lá? ii Ao meio-dia.
   c Você mora em Londres?   iii Vou de ônibus.
   d A que horas come o almoço?   iv Não, vou a um café.
   e Você come no escritório?   v   Não, moro em Manchester.

Do you understand?

People do all kinds of work. Look at these advertisements overleaf, and see if you can answer these questions.

1 Luci is a fortune-teller – true or false?

2 What language must you speak to get the au pair's job?

3 Which advertisement would you answer if you needed some sewing doing?

4 Who can help you if you are suffering from stress?

5 The 26-year-old Brazilian girl would like to be a teacher – true or false?

6 Where might you apply for a job if you enjoyed driving?

a

Gina, massagista terapêutica

KIRODRENAGEM

Trata: celulite, gorduras localizadas, dores, stress. Atende a domicílio Para marcar hora ligue 371330

b

Brasileira

26 anos, 1,56m, falando espanhol, inglês, gostaria de realizar seu grande sonho como atriz, dançarina de samba, lambada, etc. Favor contatar 0389667

c

TARÔ & TRABALHOS ESPIRITUAIS

Se você tem problemas, consulte Luci 484949

d

Costuras em geral:

Coletas para garçons Reformas, etc. **6900372**

e

AEROPORTO

- Motoristas profissionais
- Carros novos e confortáveis
- Eficiência e pontualidade
- Serviço de classe

A partir de R$ 26

Tel: 1388926

f

Procura-se AU PAIR

que fale português, para nos ajudar com a casa e o nosso filho de 4 anos. Fins de semana livres. Fale com Lucila **568221**

06

o que faz no tempo livre?

what do you do in your free time?

In this unit you will learn
- how to talk about leisure time
- how to discuss what you like doing
- how to talk about leisure facilities and entertainment

▶ Dialogue 1

Sylvia and the Ferreiras discuss their favourite leisure activities.

José   Sylvia, o que você faz no seu tempo livre?

Sylvia   Adoro ler. Durante a semana, quando volto do trabalho, gosto muito de escutar um pouco de música, e ler um bom livro.

José   Que tipo de livros prefere?

Sylvia   Prefiro os livros policiais, mas também leio muitos jornais.

Marli   E qual é a música de que você gosta mais?

Sylvia   Gosto da música latina, mas para relaxar ouço música clássica.

Marli   Vai adorar a música popular brasileira – é ótima para dançar.

Sylvia   Vocês, o que fazem nas horas vagas?

José   Aos fins de semana costumamos passar tempo no clube – nadando, jogando tênis, relaxando no bar. Pessoalmente gosto de jogar golfe, mas Marli não gosta.

Marli   É verdade, eu prefiro fazer cooper bem cedo de manhã, e aos domingos pratico ioga.

Sylvia   E a televisão? As famosas telenovelas brasileiras?

Marli   Só quando não temos mais nada a fazer.

o que você/s faz/em?	*what do you do?*
o tempo livre/horas vagas	*free/leisure time*
adoro/gosto	*I love/like*
ler	*to read*
quando	*when*
volto/leio/ouço	*I return/read/listen*
ouvir/escutar	*hear/listen to*
a música latina/clássica	*latin/classical music*
a música popular brasileira	*Brazilian pop music*
livro (o)	*book*
que tipo de	*what kind of*
prefere/prefiro	*s/he prefers/I prefer*
policiais	*police*
jornais (os)	*newspapers*
relaxar/dançar	*to relax/dance*
vai adorar	*you're going to love*
ótimo/a	*great*
aos fins de semana	*at weekends*
aos domingos	*on Sundays*
costumamos	*we usually*

passar tempo	to spend time
clube (o)	social club
nadando/relaxando	swimming/relaxing
jogando tênis	playing tennis
bar (o)	bar
pessoalmente	personally
não gosta	s/he does not like
golfe (o)	golf
é verdade	it's true
fazer cooper	to go jogging
bem cedo	really early
pratico ioga	I do yoga
televisão (a)	TV
as famosas telenovelas brasileiras	the famous Brazilian soap operas
mais nada a fazer	nothing else to do

Exercise

Say which activities the characters from the dialogue do and don't like doing.

		reading	sports	television	music
a	Marli				
b	José				
c	Sylvia				

Grammar

Activity vocabulary

Here are some words you will find useful in order to discuss leisure activities.

Verbs	
jogar tênis/futebol/vôlei/golfe	to play tennis/football/ volleyball/golf
passear	to go strolling
correr/fazer cooper	to run/go jogging

pintar	*to paint*
ler livros/revistas/jornais	*to read books/magazines/ newspapers*
escutar música	*to listen to music*
nadar	*to swim*

Nouns	
a piscina	*swimming pool*
o clube	*social/sport club*
o museu	*museum*
o rádio/a TV	*radio/TV*
o centro esportivo	*sports centre*
o cinema	*cinema*
o teatro	*theatre*
o campo	*countryside*

Likes/dislikes/preferences

Some important verbs to express your likes and dislikes are:

gostar (de)	*to like*
não gostar (de)	*not to like*
adorar	*to adore*
detestar	*to detest*
preferir	*to prefer*
gostar mais (de)	*to like most/more*

When talking about activities, all these verbs are followed by an infinitive. Be careful with the *I* person of **preferir**: it is **prefiro**. For example:

Prefiro ler.	*I prefer reading/to read.*
Adoro jogar golfe.	*I love playing/to play golf.*
Lúcia prefere ver televisão.	*Lucia prefers to watch/ watching TV.*
João gosta mais de nadar.	*John likes to swim/ swimming most.*

Gostar (de) To like

Gostar is always followed by **de**, although this does not add anything useful to the meaning. If the verb is used with a noun, you must remember to combine the **de** with words like **o, a, um, uma** etc. if appropriate. For example:

Gostamos de pintar.	*We like to paint/painting.*
Gosto do sol.	*I like the sun.*
Ele gosta mais da cerveja.	*He likes the beer most.*

Irregular plurals

Nouns and adjectives which end in -l in the singular have irregular endings, as you saw in the dialogue:

o jornal – jorna*is*
policial – policia*is*

Be on the look-out for others as you develop your reading skills.

More irregular verbs

Some more important verbs with irregularities.

fazer *to do, make*	**ler** *to read*	**ouvir** *to hear*
faço	leio	ouço
faz	lê	ouve
fazemos	lemos	ouvimos
fazem	lêem	ouvem

▶ Time routines

The days of the week are:

segunda-feira	*Monday*	**sexta-feira**	*Friday*
terça-feira	*Tuesday*	**sábado**	*Saturday*
quarta-feira	*Wednesday*	**domingo**	*Sunday*
quinta-feira	*Thursday*		

The weekdays are all feminine, whilst the week-end days are masculine. Often -**feira** is dropped, people referring simply to **segunda** etc. They are abbreviated thus: 2a, 3a, etc. To say when you do certain activities, you can say:

aos (nos) sábados / aos (nos)   on *Saturdays/Sundays/*
  domingos/ao (no) fim de semana   *at the weekend*
às (nas) segundas, terças etc.   on *Mondays, Tuesdays, etc.*
todos/as os/as   *every*

-ando -ing

The Portuguese equivalent of the *-ing* form of verbs is formed thus: verb in infinitive minus the ending (-ar/-er/-ir) + -ando/-endo/-indo. For example:

escutar *to listen (to)* escut- + -ando = escutando *listening to*

> Ele prefere ficar em casa   *He prefers to stay at home*
>   escutando música.   *listening to music.*

BUT to say *I like swimming* you must still use the structure mentioned earlier with the verb *to like* – gostar de/adorar + infinitive, e.g. gosto de nadar *I like swimming/to swim.*

▶ Dialogue 2

The Ferreiras take Sylvia out to a local bar.

José	Quer provar uma bebida nacional, Sylvia?
Sylvia	O que é?
José	É caipirinha. Sabe o que é?
Sylvia	Não faço ideia.
Marli	É uma delícia – feita de cachaça, um aguardente de cana de açúcar, com limão, açúcar e água. É um bocado forte.
Sylvia	Então, por que não?
José	Garçom, por favor.
Garçom	Pois não?
José	Duas caipirinhas e uma batida de morango.
Garçom	Muito bem.
Marli	Sylvia, você vai ao teatro em Manchester?
Sylvia	De vez em quando sim. Prefiro ir ao cinema quando surge a oportunidade. Há bons teatros aqui?
Marli	Ah, sim, aqui em São Paulo há muitos – cinemas e teatros com todo tipo de peça – comédia/romance/musical – só que em alguns os ingressos são bastante caros.
José	Em São Paulo há coisas para todo mundo – cinema, teatro, museu, discoteca, galeria de arte – há de tudo.

quer provar?	*do you want to try?*
bebida (a)	*drink*
nacional	*national*
o que é?	*what is it?*
caipirinha (a)	*sugar cane/lime drink*
não faço ideia	*I've no idea*
uma delícia	*delicious*
cachaça, aguardente	*firewater*
limão (o)	*lime*
água (a)	*water*
pois não?	*can I help you?*
uma batida de morango	*strawberry/wine cocktail*
quando surge a oportunidade	*when the opportunity arises*
de vez em quando	*sometimes*
peça (a)	*play*
ingressos (os)	*tickets*
caro/s	*expensive*
todo mundo	*everyone*
discoteca (a)	*disco*
há de tudo	*there's a bit of everything*
um bocado forte	*a bit strong*

True or false?

Are the following sentences **verdadeiras** or **falsas**?

V   F

a   Caipirinha is an alcoholic drink.
b   Sylvia never goes to the theatre.
c   São Paulo has a wide range of activities.

Grammar

Querer To want

When asking someone if they would like something, you can either say **quer** (lit. *do you want*), or **queria** (*would you like*). Despite the latter being considered more polite in English, it is not considered rude to use **quer**. Here are the two forms in full:

quero	*I want*	queria	*I would like*
quer	*you, s/he want(s)*	queria	*you would like, he, she, etc.*
queremos	*we want*	queríamos	*we would like*
querem	*you/they want*	queriam	*you/they would like*

'To know' or 'to know'?

There are two verbs for *to know* in Portuguese – **saber** is *to know a fact* or *how to do something*; **conhecer** is *to know a person, place* and *to meet, get to know someone*.

sei	conheço
sabe	conhece
sabemos	conhecemos
sabem	conhecem

e.g. **Que horas são? Não sei.**   *What time is it? I don't know.*
     Ela conhece meu filho.   *She knows my son.*

Some ...

The full version is:

algum	alguma	alguns	algumas

You can also use:

um	uma	uns	umas

Algum, etc. can be contracted with **em** (**nalgum**) and **de** (**dalgum**), although you will rarely come across these forms in Brazil.

Study these examples:

Algumas (umas) pessoas trabalham muito.   *Some people work a lot.*
Não gosto de entrar em alguns (nalguns) bares.   *I don't like going in to some bars.*

i Many alcoholic drinks in Brazil take as their base the delicious tropical fruits available there. **Batidas** are cocktails of wine, red or white, blended with a fruit – favourites are **batida de coco** *coconut*, **morango** *strawberry*, **maracujá** *passion fruit*, **pêssego** *peach*. **Caipirinha** is very potent and easily addictive! Lime and sugar are mixed with firewater, commonly referred to as **pinga** or **cachaça**, and is extremely easy to drink in copious amounts. Be careful – it has a kick! During the February carnival many people take to the streets with cans filled with pure **pinga** tied around their necks. No wonder they keep the samba going for five days!

Summary

o que faz/em no seu tempo livre/horas vagas?	*what do you do in your free leisure time?*
gosto muito de ler/escutar música	*I like reading/listening to music a lot*
que prefere?	*what do you prefer?*
prefiro ...	*I prefer ...*
costumo/costumamos ...	*I/we usually ...*
aos domingos/às segundas	*on Sundays/Mondays*
você vai ao teatro/cinema?	*do you go to the theatre/ cinema?*
de vez em quando/às vezes	*sometimes*
há bons teatros/museus aqui?	*are there any good theatres/ museums here?*
há de tudo	*there's a bit of everything*

Practice

1   Link up the pictures of the activities with what the bubbles are describing.

i Gosto de visitar o museu

ii Paulo adora jogar tênis

a

b

iii Gostamos muito de ouvir música

iv Ana prefere ler

v Adoro nadar

2 Saber or conhecer?

Place the correct form of the appropriate verb in the spaces.

a Eu _____ a França muito bem.
b Miguel não _____ nadar.
c A que horas vamos ao cinema? Eu não _____.
d Sonia, você _____ Senhor Veloso?
e Eles não _____ esta cidade.

3 ▶ Listen to three people (speakers 1, 2 and 3) discussing what they like doing in their leisure time, and decide which profile below belongs to which person.

a likes painting, museums and playing golf
b prefers watching TV, doesn't like sports
c likes golf and tennis but doesn't like music

4 Fill in your part of the dialogue about leisure time.

Francisco	O que você faz no seu tempo livre?
You	(say *I love swimming, I go to the swimming pool on Saturdays*).
Francisco	E você gosta de música?
You	(say *yes, a little*)
Francisco	Que tipo de música prefere?
You	(say *I prefer jazz music. Ask Francisco what he does in his free time.*)
Francisco	Bom, gosto muito de jogar golfe, e de ir ao teatro.
You	(say *I also like the theatre but the tickets are quite expensive.*)

Do you understand?

1 Below is some information about courses you can do at a local college. Paulo has chosen a course on gardening. Look at how he has filled in his request form, then choose a course yourself, and fill in the blank form with personal details.

Electrônica básica radiotécnica e (áudio televisão p.b. e em cores)		Silk-screen	Golfe	Espanhol
		Desenho artístico e publicitário	violão	Mecânica de automóveis
Corte e costura	Fotografia	Electricidade	Electricidade de automóveis	Auxiliar de escritório
Auxiliar de contabilidado	Auxiliar em administração de empresas	Tricô	Bordado e crochê	Beleza de mulher
Secretariado moderno	Jardinagem	Vinhos	Mestre de obras (edificações)	Natação
Mecânica geral	Mecânica de motos	Refrigeração e ar condicionado	Desenho de mecânica	Desenho arquitetônico
Especialização em videocassette	Técnicas vendas	Informática	Inglês	Caligrafia

INSTITUTO UNIVERSAL BRASILEIRO SP
Av. Rio Branco, 781 – Caixa Postal 5058 – São Paulo – CEP 01061-970

Sr. Diretor, peço Grátis o folheto sobre o(s) curso(s) profissionalizante(s)

livre(s) de ___*Jardinagem*___ ◄——————— COURSE

NOME ___*Paulo de Oliveira Martins*___

RUA ___*Julieta Mesquita*___ N° _*35*_

POST CODE ► CEP _*01326*_ BAIRRO _*Centro*_ CX. POSTAL ___ ◄—— MAIL BOX No.

CIDADE _*Belo Horizonte*_ ▲ ESTADO _*Minas*_

DISTRICT

INSTITUTO UNIVERSAL BRASILEIRO SP

Av. Rio Branco, 781 – Caixa Postal 5058 – São Paulo – CEP 01061-970

Sr. Diretor, peço Grátis o folheto sobre o(s) curso(s) profissionalizante(s) livre(s) de _____

NOME _____

RUA _____ Nº _____

CEP _____ BAIRRO _____ CX. POSTAL _____

CIDADE _____ ESTADO _____

2 Which courses would you choose if you wanted to study:

a The guitar
b General mechanics
c Art and design

07

pois não?

can I help you?

In this unit you will learn
- how to obtain goods and services
- how to buy clothes and shoes
- how to discuss sizes

▶ Dialogue 1

Sylvia has gone to visit Rio and decides to do some shopping in a fashion store (**a boutique**) before starting her journey northwards.

Empregada	Pois não?
Sylvia	Queria ver umas camisetas, por favor.
Empregada	Claro. Qual é o seu tamanho?
Sylvia	É o 42.
Empregada	Você procura uma cor em particular?
Sylvia	Tem em verde, ou azul?
Empregada	Sim, temos estas aqui, e também aquelas ali em outro estilo. São todas de algodão.
Sylvia	Posso provar?
Empregada	Claro – a cabine de provas é ali ao fundo.

(*Sylvia comes out of the changing room.*)

Empregada	Então, já escolheu?
Sylvia	Acho que sim. Vou levar esta azul, mas tem a outra em verde-escuro?
Empregada	Neste momento não, sinto muito.
Sylvia	Não faz mal. Levo as duas. Quanto é?
Empregada	São 36 reais ao todo. Quer pagar ali na caixa? Leve este talão consigo. Depois volte aqui para pegar as camisetas.
Sylvia	Obrigada.

Pois não?	*Can I help you?*
camisetas (as)	*t-shirts*
claro	*of course*
tamanho (o)	*size*
você procura ...?	*are you looking for ...?*
uma cor em particular	*a particular colour*
estilo (o)	*style*
posso provar?	*may I try it on?*
a cabine de provas	*changing room*
ao fundo	*at the bottom, end*
já escolheu?	*have you chosen yet?*
acho que sim	*I think so*
vou levar	*I'll take*
neste momento	*at the moment*
sinto muito	*I'm sorry*
não faz mal	*that's OK*
quanto é?	*how much is it/that?*

ao todo	*in all*
pagar	*to pay for*
caixa (a)	*till/check-out*
leve/volte	*take/return*
talão (o)	*ticket/stub*
consigo	*with you*

Exercise 1

Only one of these statements is true. Which one?

a   O tamanho da Sylvia é quarenta e quatro.
b   A cabine de provas é à esquerda.
c   Sylvia leva duas camisetas.

Grammar

Posso ...? May I ...?

Posso *may I/can I* can be used with all kinds of verbs in the infinitive, and is very useful. **Posso ver?** *see, have a look?* **Posso experimentar, provar?** *to try on, try something, taste?* **Posso passar?** *to pass, get by?* The verb is **poder** *to be able to* and in full is:

posso	podemos
pode	podem

I think so

The verb **achar** has various meanings *to find, think*. It can be used when asking/giving opinions:

> **Acho que sim/não.** *I think so/not.*
> **O que você acha?** *What do you think?*
> **Acho muito bonito.** *I think (it's) very pretty.*

You can also use **creio que** *I believe* and **penso que** *I think*.

Levo I'll take

Levo is in fact the present tense of the verb even though in English we are saying *I will take* (i.e. future). This replacement of a future action with a verb in the present tense is very common in Portuguese, especially in spoken dialogue. For example:

Amanhã vejo meu irmão. *Tomorrow I'll see my brother.*
Falamos a semana que vem. *We'll talk next week.*

As in English, you can also use the verb *to go* (**ir**) to express future action. For example:

Vou à cidade amanhã. *I'm going to town tomorrow.*

The future tense will be introduced later in the course.

Leve..., *volte ...*: commands

In Unit 4, you learnt how to give directions, politely telling people what to do by saying *you (do) this/that.* There are also other ways of ordering people to do things more directly. These are called *commands*, or more technically *imperatives*. Remember that you do not need to be annoyed with someone in order to command them to do or not do something. To form the commands, look at the following steps:

-**ar** verbs: **comprar**	-**er** verbs: **comer**	-**ir** verbs: **partir**
(**você**) **compra** = *you buy*	**come** = *you eat*	**parte** = *you leave*

To form the command change the verb endings to the following:

compre! = *buy!*   **coma!** = *eat!*   **parta!** = *leave!*

There is a crossing-over of endings – the -**ar** verbs take an -**e**, and the -**er**/-**ir** verbs take an -**a**. To command more than one person, add an -**m**. For example:

(**vocês**) **comprem!**   **comam!**   **partam!**

To tell somebody *not* to do something, simply place **não** in front – **não coma!** *don't eat!* Be careful with irregular verbs: here is a small selection of some you have already come across:

fazer	faça!	façam!
ver	veja!	vejam!
ir	vá!	vão!
vir	venha!	venham!
pedir	peça!	peçam!

Be on the look-out for irregular verbs, but don't expect to take them on board all at once. They are particularly tricky in Portuguese, and take time to learn.

▶ Dialogue 2

Sylvia next goes to a shoe shop – **a sapataria.**

Sylvia	Bom dia. Queria ver uns sapatos em couro, por favor. Tem?
Empregada	Sim, temos. Que número é que você calça?
Sylvia	Acho que é o 38, mas não tenho certeza.
Empregada	Bom, em 38 temos estes, que estão muito na moda agora.
Sylvia	Sim, são muito bonitos, mas queria alguma coisa mais resistente – para andar.
Empregada	Temos estas botas, que são cómodas, e estão em liquidação esta semana.
Sylvia	Posso experimentar?
Empregada	Claro. Tome!
Sylvia	São muito pequenas. Tem outras maiores?
Empregada	Sim, aqui em 39.
Sylvia	Ah, sim, estas são mais cómodas. O que você acha?
Empregada	Apesar de ser resistentes, também é 'chique'. Ficam-lhe bem.
Sylvia	Quanto custam?
Empregada	Com o desconto, custam 85 reais.
Sylvia	Que pechincha!

sapatos (os)	shoes
couro (o)	leather
tem?	do you have?
que número ... calça?	what size do you take?
não tenho certeza	I'm not sure
estar na moda	to be in fashion
resistente	solid/firm
andar	to walk
botas (as)	boots
cómodas	comfortable
em liquidação	in the sale
são muito pequenas	they're too small
apesar de ser	in spite of being
chique	chic
ficam-lhe bem	they suit you
quanto custa/m	how much does it/do they cost?
desconto (o)	discount
que pechincha	what a bargain

Exercise 2

Answer three questions in Portuguese, based on the dialogue.

a O que a Sylvia quer comprar? _____
b Qual é o número das botas que ela compra? _____
c Quanto custam? _____

Grammar

Clothes check-list

a blusa	blouse	a camisa	shirt
as calças	trousers	o vestido	dress
a saia	skirt	a cueca	underpants
a calcinha	knickers	o sutiã	bra
as meias	socks	as sandálias	sandals
as luvas	gloves	o chapéu	hat

Materials

algodão	cotton	poliéster	polyester
couro	leather	plástico	plastic
lã	wool	seda	silk
cetim	satin	malha	jersey/knitwear

Shops

Often the name of a shop is derived from the item sold there.

sapatos	shoes	sapataria	shoeshop
pão	bread	padaria	baker's
livro	book	livraria	bookshop
pastel	pastry, cake	pastelaria	cakeshop
tabaco	tobacco	tabacaria	tobacconist's
fruta	fruit	frutaria	fruiterer

Summary

Queria/posso ... ver/ provar/experimentar?	I woud like to/may I ... see/ try on/try?
Qual tamanho/que número calça?	What size do you take?

Portuguese	English
Em que cor?	*In which colour?*
Tem .../tem em ...?	*Do you have/do you have in ...?*
Quanto é/quanto custa/m?	*How much is it/does it/ they cost?*
Levo/vou levar	*I'll take/I'm going to take*
Acho que	*I think that*
É/são muito pequeno/s, grande/s	*It is/they are too small/large*
Fica/m-lhe bem	*It/they suit you*

i Rio is a city of great contrasts. It is arguably one of the most beautiful cities in the world, with its breathtaking scenery and renowned beaches. But there is also great poverty in the shantytowns (**as favelas**). Many will have heard of the police death squads hired by business people to rid the streets of the children who sleep rough. Rio is everything from squalor to extravagance, but it all comes together for its magnificent February carnival – **o carnaval**. Do be careful in Rio – exercise caution when out and about, but don't be too afraid to enjoy its beauty. And don't be shocked by the amount of flesh shown on the beach. Brazilian women don't often sunbathe topless, but their bikinis reveal an awful lot of flesh. Often referred to as 'fio dental' bikinis (dental floss!), they leave little to the imagination. Tone up before you venture on to Copacabana, Ipanema and Leblon!

Practice

1 Match up the items to be bought with the appropriate shops.

i livraria	ii sapataria	iii mercado	iv açougue
	v boutique	vi padaria	

2 Supply your part of the dialogue in a fashion store

You	(Say *do you have skirts?*)
Empregada	Sim, temos. Qual é seu tamanho?
You	(Say *I think it's 42*)
Empregada	Temos estas, em vermelho e preto.
You	(Say *do you have it in light-blue?*)
Empregada	Sim, temos esta, em outro estilo.
You	(Say *how much is it?*)
Empregada	Esta custa 46 reais
You	(Say *I'll take this one in blue and that one in black.*)
Empregada	São 92 reais ao todo.
You	(Say *thank you.*)

3 Fill in the gaps by supplying the correct command form of the verb. Then say what each one means.

a (você) [comprar] _____ a blusa! _____
b (vocês) [comer] _____ o pão! _____
c (vocês) [ir] _____ por aqui! _____
d (você) [não fazer] _____ barulho! _____
e (você) [trabalhar] _____ bem! _____
f (vocês) [não falar] _____ muito! _____

4 ▶ Listen to someone in a shoe shop, and tick the appropriate pictures for their purchases.

a Asks for

b Size

c Colour   black   brown   green

d Do they fit?

e Price

Do you understand?

Look at the advice given to people under their horoscope and answer the following:

1 What should Pisces be eating?
2 What culinary advice is given to Cancer?
3 What should Libra do for their friends?
4 What should Capricorn do on arriving home?
5 What should Aries do before taking a decision?
6 What should Leo treat themselves to?

HORÓSCOPO

PREVISÕES PARA O PERÍODO DE 28 DE DEZEMBRO A 28 DE JANEIRO

CAPRICÓRNIO
22 DEZ. a 20 JAN.
Dica: Quando chegar em casa tome um bom banho de sais.

AQUÁRIO
21 JAN. a 19 FEV.
Dica: Que tal um novo corte de cabelo? Você vai se sentir outra …

PEIXES
20 FEV. a 20 MAR.
Dica: Abuse das saladas. Elas irao manter seu bom humor no verão.

ÁRIES
21 MAR. a 20 ABRIL
Dica: Relaxe muito antes de tomar qualquer decisão.

TOURO
21 ABRIL a 20 MAIO
Dica: Gente. Isso é tudo o que você precisa para melhorar sua vida.

GÊMEOS
21 MAIO a 20 JUNHO
Dica: Não fique apenas pensando em cursos. Faça a matrícula já!

CÂNCER
21 JUNHO a 21 JULHO
Dica: Troque os doces por frutas. Seus dentes vão agradecer.

LEÃO
22 JULHO a 22 AGO.
Dica: Procure uma boa mão oriental e entregue-se às massagens.

VIRGEM
23 AGO. a 22 SET.
Dica: Aposte nos melhores produtos de beleza. Eles vão te ajudar.

LIBRA
23 SET. a 22 OUT.
Dica: Faça um jantar para os seus amigos e ponha um sorriso no rosto, menina.

ESCORPIÃO
23 OUT. a 21 NOV.
Dica: O sol chegou! Aproveite para colocar o bronzeado em dia também.

SAGITÁRIO
22 NOV. a 21 DEZ.
Dica: Viagens à vista. Não tenha medo. Arrume as malas para voar linda.

08

que vai comer?
what are you going to eat?

In this unit you will learn
- how to order a meal
- more about making requests
- about typical Brazilian food

▶ Dialogue 1

Sylvia goes out to a restaurant with a friend.

Márcia	Tem uma mesa livre?
Garçom	São quantos?
Márcia	Somos só dois.
Garçom	Temos esta mesa aqui perto da porta, ou aquela ali ao fundo.
Márcia	Esta está bem. Traga o cardápio por favor.
Garçom	Tome.
Márcia	Deixe ver. O que temos? Há saladas e sopas para começar. Que vai pedir, Sylvia?
Sylvia	Não tenho muita fome. Quero uma sopa quentinha.
Márcia	A canja é boa e típica daqui. É feita de galinha.
Sylvia	Então é isto para mim.
Márcia	Eu vou pedir uma salada mista para mim.

mesa (a)	table
livre	free
são quantos?	how many of you are there?
somos ...	there are ... of us
porta (a)	door
traga	bring
cardápio (o)	menu
tome	here you are/take
deixe ver	let (me) see
saladas/salada mista	salads/mixed salad
sopas/sopa quentinha	soups/hot soup
para começar	to start with
não tenho muita fome	I'm not very hungry
canja (a)	chicken broth
típica daqui	typical of here
galinha (a)	chicken
é isto para mim	I'll have this

Exercise 1

Say if these statements are **verdadeiro** or **falso**.

V   F

a They choose a table near the door.
b Sylvia is really hungry.
c Márcia chooses soup as a starter.

Grammar

Traga! Bring!

This command comes from the verb **trazer** *to bring*. In the last unit you were advised to keep a look-out for verbs with irregularities, and here is an example of a verb whose irregularity affects the command-form: **trago, traz, trazemos, trazem.** The command becomes **Traga!** *Bring!*

In addition to those listed in Unit 7, other verbs which act in the same way include:

seguir *to follow*	sigo segue seguimos seguem	siga!
repetir *to repeat*	repito repete repetimos repetem	repita!
dormir *to sleep*	durmo dorme dormimos dormem	durma!

Há ... There is/there are ...

This small word which you met in Unit 4 for directions is extremely versatile. It means *there is/there are*, and when used as a question, also means *is there? are there?* It is particularly useful when requesting information about what is available: **o que há?** *what is there?* You can also say **o que tem?** *what do you have?*

Ter in special expressions

The verb **ter** (*to have*) is used in certain expressions such as **tenho fome** *I am hungry*: **ter fome** *to be hungry* (literally to *have hunger*).

You will also come across

ter	**sede**	*to be thirsty*
	sono	*to be sleepy/tired*
	calor	*to be hot*
	frio	*to be cold*

You can also use **estar com** + **fome, sede,** etc.

Dialogue 2

The waiter takes the order.

Garçom   Então, já escolheram? Que vão comer?
Sylvia   Para começar, uma salada mista e uma canja.
Garçom   E depois?
Sylvia   Um lombo assado e um filé de peixe frito com batatas fritas, arroz e legumes para dois.
Garçom   E para beber?
Sylvia   Uma garrafa do vinho da casa.
Garçom   Branco ou tinto?
Sylvia   Branco. E traga uma jarra de água também por favor – tenho muita sede.
Garçom   Muito bem.

já escolheram?	*have you* (pl.) *chosen yet?*
um lombo assado	*roast pork loin*
um filé de peixe frito	*fried fish fillet*
batatas fritas	*chips*
arroz (o)	*rice*
legumes (os)	*vegetables*
garrafa (a)	*bottle*
o vinho da casa	*house wine*
tinto	*red (wine)*
jarra (a)	*jug*

Exercise 2

Answer 'yes' or 'no'.

                                YES   **NO**

a   Do they order vegetables for both of them?
b   Do they ask for red wine?
c   Is Sylvia thirsty?

Dialogue 3

The meal continues.

Márcia	Garçom, por favor!
Garçom	Diga.
Márcia	Pode trazer mais pão e outra jarra de água, por favor?
Garçom	Claro. Vão querer sobremesas?
Sylvia	O que tem?
Garçom	Hoje temos pudim de caramelo, doce de coco, fruta, e sorvete.
Márcia	Que sabores de sorvete tem?
Garçom	Chocolate, morango, baunilha e avelã.
Márcia	Bom, eu quero um sorvete de morango.
Sylvia	Eu vou provar o pudim.
Garçom	E café?
Márcia	Sim, dois cafezinhos.

pode trazer	*can you bring*	**sorvete (o)**	*ice cream*
mais pão	*more bread*	**sabores (os)**	*flavours*
sobremesas (as)	*desserts*	**chocolate**	*chocolate*
hoje	*today*	**morango**	*strawberry*
pudim de caramelo	*creme caramel*	**baunilha**	*vanilla*
doce de coco	*coconut dessert*	**avelã**	*hazelnut*
fruta	*fruit*		

Dialogue 4

Paying the bill.

Márcia	A conta, por favor.
Garçom	Aqui está.
Sylvia	Quanto é, Márcia?
Márcia	São 36 reais.
Sylvia	Tome aqui.
Márcia	Imagine! Pago eu! Insisto. Você é minha convidada.
Sylvia	Bom, a próxima vez eu pago. Obrigada. Foi um jantar delicioso. Mas já é tarde. São nove e meia, e amanhã parto para o nordeste.

foi um jantar delicioso	it was a delicious dinner
conta (a)	bill
pago eu	I'll pay
insisto	I insist
minha convidada	my guest
a próxima vez	next time
já é tarde	it's already late
o nordeste	the northeast
imagine!	get away/never!

Summary

Tem uma mesa livre?	*Do you have a table free?*
Traga o cardápio, por favor	*Please bring the menu.*
Que vai pedir/comer?	*What are you going to have/eat?*
O que há/tem? Há/Tem ...	*What is there/do you have? There is ...*
Tenho fome/sede.	*I'm hungry/thirsty.*
Para começar/c depois/ para beber	*For starters/and then/to drink*
Pode trazer mais .../outro/a ...	*Can you bring more .../ another ...*
Que sabores?	*What flavours?*
A conta, por favor.	*The bill please.*
Foi um (jantar) delicioso.	*It was a delicious (dinner).*

i The Brazilians' main staple of food is rice and black beans – **arroz e feijão**, usually eaten with steak **um filé** and chips and salad. You can hear the beans cooking away all day in pressure cookers down many residential streets. When eating out, popular choices include Italian food (there is a huge Italian community in and around São Paulo); chicken (**frango**) and fish (**peixe**). Sunday is the day for the infamous black bean stew cooked with all kinds of sausage and off-cuts – **feijoada**. Sometimes it's better not to enquire what every bit is! It is served with rice, **couve à mineira** (sauté greens) and **farofa** – a breadcrumb mixture (**manioc**), and also a slice of orange to aid digestion. In the south you are more likely to eat in a **churrascaria-rodízio** – a sort of organized barbecue, where waiters circle the tables with swordsful of every meat you can imagine. As your plate empties you simply catch the waiters' attention. There is usually a help-yourself salad bar, and normally you pay one price and eat until you burst. This is particularly popular in the **gaúcho** – cowboy-regions of the south. More about these later in the course.

Meals are leisurely affairs, unless you are working – but even here many a deal has been clinched over an extended lunch.

Typical Brazilian food

Entradas – *starters*

canja	*chicken broth*	**lula frita**	*fried squid*
creme de		**camarão**	*prawns*
aspargos	*asparagus soup*		

Prato principal – *main meal*

lombo assado	*roast pork loin*	**massa**	*pasta*
frango ensopado	*chicken stew*	**espeto misto**	*mixed kebab*
ovelha	*lamb*	**bife na brasa**	*barbecued steak*

Guarnições – *side dishes*

arroz	*rice*	**batatas fritas**	*chips*
legumes	*vegetables*	**farofa**	*manioc mixture*

Sobremesas – *desserts*

sorvetes	*ice cream*	**pudim de caramelo**	*creme caramel*
fruta	*fruit*	**doce de coco**	*coconut dessert*

Bebidas – *drinks*

refrigerantes	*soft drinks*	**vinho**	*wine*
cerveja	*beer*		

Practice

1 Can you do the following?

  a Say *do you have a table free?*
  b Say *there are five of us.*
  c Say *I'm not thirsty.*
  d Ask your friend what s/he is going to have.
  e Call the waiter across.
  f Ask for the bill.

2 Place an appropriate command from the box below into the spaces.

  a Para o museu? _____ por esta rua!
  b _____ favor!
  c Não _____ todo o vinho!

d _____ a frase!
e Não _____ tão rápido!
f Por favor, _____ mais água!

traga   beba   sigam   coma   falem   faça   repitam

3 Use the food lists above to help you complete your part of this dialogue.

Garçom   Então, já escolheu? Que vai comer?
You   (say *to start, a vegetable soup*)
Garçom   E depois?
You   (say *lamb with rice and salad*)
Garçom   E para beber?
You   (say *a beer and a jug of water*)
Garçom   Muito bem.

4 ▶ Listen to the dialogue about desserts and fill in the gaps with the missing words.

A Vão querer _____?
B O que tem?
A _____ temos fruta, _____, e pudim.
B Que sabores de sorvete tem?
A Chocolate, _____, e avelã.
B Bom, eu quero um de _____.
A E café?
B _____ um cafezinho.

5 Fill in the bubbles with the correct form of the verb **ter**, plus the word which describes what the people in the pictures are feeling.

a Eu …   b Ana …   c Nós …
d Você …?   e Eles …

6 Look at the various bills from restaurants, and match them to the amounts paid below.

i 97 R $ ii 145 R $ iii 63 R $ iv 118 R $

a sessenta e três reais
b cento e quarenta e cinco reais
c noventa e sete reais
d cento e dezoito reais

7 Indicate where the following food and drink items would appear on a menu, by ticking the appropriate columns.

		starter	main meal	side dish	dessert	drink
a	sorvete					
b	água					
c	café					
d	sopa					
e	bife					
f	legumes					
g	camarão					
h	farofa					

Do you understand?

Look at the following menu, then the preference of the people dining out with you. Choose a 3-course meal suitable for all concerned.

Laura is a vegetarian and cannot eat sugar.

Marcelo hates fish/seafood but loves to eat white meat. He loves coconuts.

Sérgio is allergic to shrimps and doesn't like starting a meal with soup. He enjoys eating a mixture of meats in a main meal, and loves very sweet desserts.

You can't manage a starter, but can get through a good steak. You prefer ice-cream for afters.

Rita is very traditional, and likes to start her meal with good, hot broth, followed by fish and likes something fresh for dessert.

Restaurante o Paraná

Cardápio

Entradas

Camarão a Paulista
Creme de aspargos
Lula Frita
Canja

Prato Principal

Bife na Brasa
Frango assado
Peixe à minuana
Ovelha na Brasa
Espeto misto
Omelete de queijo
Todos servidos com arroz,
legumes e batatas

Sobremesa

Doce de coco
Pudim de caramelo
Sorvetes e Sorbet
Fruta

	Starter	Main Meal	Dessert
Laura			
Marcelo			
Sérgio			
You			
Rita			

09

vai viajar?

are you going travelling?

In this unit you will learn
- how to use public transport
- how to ask for change
- how to find out departure and arrival times

▶ Dialogue 1

Sylvia decides to travel northwards to the cities of Salvador and Fortaleza in the **nordeste**. She needs a taxi to get to the coach station. Listen to her conversation at the taxi rank (**o ponto de táxi**).

Sylvia	Pode me levar à estação rodoviária, por favor?
Motorista	Posso, sim, sem problema. Vai viajar?
Sylvia	Sim, vou para o nordeste, passar uns dias em Salvador e Fortaleza.
Motorista	Cidades bonitas. Também precisa visitar a cidade de Olinda; é muito histórica e faz parte de nosso patrimônio.
Sylvia	Vou tentar.
Motorista	Aqui estamos.
Sylvia	Quanto é?
Motorista	16 reais. Boa viagem.

pode/posso	*can you/I can*
levar	*to take*
estação (a) rodoviária	*bus station*
sem problema	*no problem*
viajar	*to travel*
passar	*to spend (time)*
precisa	*you need*
faz parte de	*it's part of*
nosso patrimônio	*our heritage*
tentar	*to try*
boa viagem	*bon voyage*

▶ Dialogue 2

Sylvia goes to the ticket office (**a bilheteria**) to purchase her coach ticket.

Sylvia	A que horas parte o próximo ônibus de luxo para Salvador?
Empregado	Parte às dez e quinze.
Sylvia	Queria um bilhete para este, se faz favor.
Empregado	De ida ou de ida e volta?
Sylvia	Só de ida.
Empregado	Muito bem. Agora, são 68 reais.
Sylvia	Tem troco para uma nota de cem reais?
Empregado	Sim, tenho. Tome.
Sylvia	Obrigada. O ônibus sai de onde?
Empregado	Sai do portão número 22. É por ali à esquerda.

o próximo	the next
bilhete (o)	ticket
de ida/de ida e volta	single/return
tem troco para?	do you have change for?
uma nota de	a ... note
sai de onde?	where does it leave from?
o portão número 22	gate no 22

Grammar

Pode me levar ...? Can you take me ...?

In Unit 1 you learnt the Portuguese words known as personal pronouns for *I*, *you*, *he*, etc. used as subjects of verbs. In the dialogue above, you were introduced to another pronoun, this time an object of the verb, i.e. one to whom (or which) the action is done directly. In English these *direct object pronouns* are: *me, you, him, her, us, them*. In Portuguese they are:

me	*me*	nos	*us*
te	*you*	os	*them, you* (pl.)
o	*him, you, it*	as	*them, you* (pl.)
a	*her, you, it*		

In English you may have examples such as *I can see you*, *you write it quickly*, *they hit us*, etc. Usually, in standard written Portuguese, these object pronouns are placed *after* the verb and attached to it by a hyphen (except in certain situations, e.g. negatives or questions). However, the Brazilians tend to place the object pronouns *before* the verb, whether in a positive or negative statement.

Eu o escrevo	*I write it* (eu escrevo-o)
Eles nos batem	*they hit us* (eles batem-nos)
Você não me vê	*you do not see me*

Often Brazilians will use the object **te** for you, instead of **o/a**, despite these latter being the correct forms corresponding to **você**. Thus: **Eu te vejo** *I see you*, and not **Eu o/a vejo**. In colloquial Portuguese, Brazilians may quite often say things like **eu vejo você** *I see you*, which is incorrect, or **eu vejo ele** *I see him* (literally *I see he*).

Nosso Our

Nosso is the remaining possessive for you to learn. Here is a reminder of the full table of possessives.

	m. sing	f. sing	m. pl.	f. pl.
eu *I*	meu	minha	meus	minhas
você *you*	seu	sua	seus	suas
ele *he*	o … dele*	a … dele	os … dele	as … dele
ela *she*	o … dela*	a … dela	os … dela	as … dela
nós *we*	nosso	nossa	nossos	nossas
vocês *you*	seu	sua	seus	suas
eles/elas	o … deles	a … deles	os … deles	as … delas
they	/delas*	/delas	/delas	/delas

* If there is no ambiguity, for all forms of *his/her/their* you can use **seu, sua**, etc. Don't forget, you will also come across examples of **o meu/a nossa**, etc. For example:

Nosso amigo	*Our friend*
A casa dele	*His house*
João é o meu amigo; sua casa é grande.	*John is my friend; his house is big.*

24-hour clock

When travelling, be aware of times given using the twenty-four hour clock. Providing you know your numbers up to 59, you should be OK. The actual structure is a simple adding process, as you learnt in Units 5 and 6.

Às dez e quinze	At 10:15
Às treze e trinta e seis	At 13:36
Às vinte e duas e quarenta e cinco	At 22:45

Dialogue 3

Having arrived in Salvador, Sylvia needs to get to the centre.

Sylvia Desculpe, senhor. O que faço para chegar ao centro da cidade?

Sr Você vai para onde exatamente?

Sylvia Não sei muito bem. Ao centro.

Sr Bem, tome o ônibus número 5A, que parte daqui, da frente da estação rodoviária, e sai na praça Vicente, que é bem no centro da cidade.

Sylvia	Obrigada. O senhor conhece um bom hotel aqui?
Sr	Sim, o hotel Beira-mar é muito bom, e não é nada caro.
Sylvia	Onde é este hotel?
Sr	É na Rua Jorge Amado, número 35.
Sylvia	Muito obrigada.
Sr	De nada.

o que faço para ...	*what do I do in order to ...*
exatamente	*exactly*
da frente de	*from in front of*
é bem ...	*it's right ...*
não é nada caro	*It's not at all expensive*

Grammar

How do I ... ?

In the dialogue, this expression was translated as **o que faço para?** (*what do I do in order to?*). You may also come across:

como se faz para ...?	*how does one ...?*
como posso ...?	*how can I ...?*

In front of: prepositions

Prepositions – words of place, location, position – are varied in Portuguese. You met some in Unit 3 which you may like to revise. Here are some more you will find useful when discovering where things are:

em frente (de)	*in front (of)*	**ao lado (de)**	*next to*
detrás/atrás (de)	*behind*	**perto (de)**	*near (to)*
debaixo (de)	*under*	**em cima (de)**	*on top (of)*
dentro (de)	*inside*	**fora (de)**	*outside*
entre	*between*	**contra**	*against*

Don't forget that if you are describing a permanent fixture, e.g. a building, you will use **ser** (*to be*) or **ficar**, but with temporary or moveable items, **estar**. For example:

O mercado é/fica perto do cinema.	*The market is near the cinema.*
Minha casa é ao lado da praça.	*My house is next to the square.*
O livro está em cima da mesa.	*The book is on top of the table.*

Summary

pode me levar a ... por favor?	*can you take me to ... please?*
vou passar uns dias em ...	*I'm going to spend a few days in ...*
precisa visitar ...	*you need to visit...*
a que horas parte/chega?	*at what time does it depart/arrive?*
o próximo trem/ ônibus (de luxo)	*the next train/coach*
queria um bilhete	*I'd like a ticket*
de ida/de ida e volta	*single/return*
tem troco para uma nota de ...?	*do you have change for a ... note?*
... sai de onde?	*from where does ... leave?*
o que faço para chegar a ...?	*how do I get to ...?*

ⓘ Transport in Brazil

Taxis are pretty cheap.

O ônibus gets very squashed in town centres, with crowds hanging off the back – wherever they can get hold. You get on at the back of many buses and have to go through a turnstyle. It's awkward if you have much luggage, but cheap.

O ônibus de luxo is for long-distance travel and inter-urban. Cheap. Some are more comfortable than others. There are frequent stops at roadside eating places, the basic equivalent of motorway stops. Also known as **ônibus-leito**, where your seat expands into a bed.

O trem is cheap but very slow. Most longer travel is preferable by coach. Probably the most infamous is the **trem da morte** – the train of death, which crosses the swamplands of the Pantanal into Bolivia.

1st/2nd class **primeira/segunda classe**;   *platform* **a linha**; *station* **a estação**

Practice

1 Insert the correct possessive word in these sentences. You may have to think first about the sentence structure in some of them.

   a Estes são [*my*] _____ sapatos [*shoes*].
   b Sonia é [*his*] _____ amiga. [careful!]
   c [*our*] _____ casa fica perto do cinema.

d [*their* f.] _____ irmãs são americanas.
e Esta é [*your* sing.] _____ chave?

2 Can you do the following?

a Say *can you take me to the town centre?*
b Wish someone a good journey.
c Ask what time the next coach to Rio departs.
d Ask if someone has change for a R$50 note.
e Ask how one gets to the Miraflores Square.
f Ask someone if they know a good restaurant here.

3 ▶ Fill in your part of the dialogue at the bus station, and practise it by listening to the cassette.

You	(Ask *what time the next coach to Fortaleza departs*)
Empregado	Parte às vinte e uma e dez.
You	(Say *you'd like a return ticket*.)
Empregado	Muito bem. São 78 reais.
You	(Ask *if he has change for a R$100 note*.)
Empregado	Sim, tenho. Tome.
You	(Ask *where the coach leaves from*.)
Empregado	Sai do portão número 11B. É aqui em frente.

4 Match up the Portuguese statements on the left with the corrrect English version on the right.

a Eu te conheço.   **i** They don't hear me.
b Eles não me ouvem.   **ii** We buy them.
c Miguel o escreve devagar. **iii** The teacher punishes us.
d A professora nos castiga. **iv** I know you.
e Nós as compramos.   **v** Miguel writes it slowly.

5 The following dialogue in a taxi has become scrambled. Can you put it in the correct order?

a Sim, vou passar uma semana em Minas.
b Aqui estamos.
c Pode me levar à estação, por favor?
d Região bonita. Precisa visitar a cidade de Ouro Preto.
e Quanto é?
f Posso, sim senhora. Vai viajar?
g Vou tentar.
h 17 reais. Obrigado.

Do you understand?

Look at the travel information below and answer T/F to these statements.

1 Ticket **a** was issued for travelling by plane.
2 With Ticket **b** you'll be travelling on a bus.
3 Ticket **c** is for a one-way journey.

a

```
Empresa Brasileira de
Infra-Estrutura
Aeroportuária


Série E      No. 279853




   TARIFA DE EMBARQUE VÔO
      DOMÉSTICO — 2a
         categoria

   Aeroporto: Salvador /
      Data: 23/05/03
```

b

c

```
Empresa Auto Ônibus Silva S/A


Rio ↔ Recife Ida e Volta / Data de emissão: 12/06/03
Preço : R$ 56,85
```

10

tem um apartamento livre?

do you have a room free?

In this unit you will learn
- how to obtain a hotel room
- how to make minor complaints
- more about Brazilian meals and meal times

▶ Dialogue 1

Sylvia approaches the Hotel Florestal in Manaus, Amazon, and enters the reception – **a recepção.**

Recepcionista	Boa tarde. Pois não?
Sylvia	Boa tarde. Tem um apartamento livre?
Recepcionista	Simples, ou duplo?
Sylvia	Simples por favor. Com banheiro.
Recepcionista	Todos os apartamentos têm banheiro. Vamos ver. É para quantos dias?
Sylvia	Para cinco dias, até quinta-feira.
Recepcionista	Bom, temos o apartamento 222 livre.
Sylvia	Quanto é por noite?
Recepcionista	58 reais, incluindo o café da manhã.
Sylvia	Está bem. Onde fica o apartamento?
Recepcionista	Fica no segundo andar, com vista para o rio. Quer preencher esta ficha antes de subir?

um apartamento livre	*a room free*
simples/duplo	*single/double*
para quantos dias?	*for how many days?*
por noite	*per night*
incluindo	*including*
o café da manhã	*breakfast*
com vista para o rio	*overlooking the river*
preencher	*to fill in*
ficha (a)	*form*
antes de subir	*before going up*

Once in her room Sylvia studies the hotel information guide (see following page).

tabela de preços	*price tariff*
c/café = com café	*with breakfast*
quarto	*room*
meia pensão	*halfboard*
pensão completa	*full board*
duas camas	*2 beds (twin)*
por pessoa	*per person*
refeições	*meals*
servem-se	*are served*
borboleta (a)	*butterfly*
a partir das ...	*from*
cama de casal	*double bed*

HOTEL
FLORESTAL

Tabela de preços:	quarto só	c/café	meia pensão	pensão completa
apartamento simples	R$40	R$58	R$75	R$95
apartamento duplo (duas camas)	R$35	R$53	R$70	R$90
apartamento duplo (cama de casal)	R$32	R$50	R$67	R$87

Preços por pessoa por noite.

Refeições (servem-se no restaurante *Borboleta*)

café da manhã	a partir das 7:30
almoço	das 12:30 até às 14:00
jantar	das 19:00 até às 21:30

Exercise 1

Can you work out the solutions to the following, based on the above hotel information?

a Mr and Mrs Johnson would like a twin room, with full board for 2 nights. How much would they pay in total?

b Are they able to have breakfast served in their room?

c If they asked to have dinner at 'seis e meia da tarde', would it be available?

Grammar

Antes de ... Before *...ing*

To say *before (or after) ...ing something*, in Portuguese you use the prepositions **antes de** *before* or **depois de** *after* plus the infinitive. For example:

antes de subir	*before going up*
depois de descer	*after going down*

You can also use other prepositions in the same way, such as **em vez de** *instead of*, **sem** *without* and **além de** *as well as*.

Servem-se refeições Meals are served

In Unit 2 you met reflexive verbs – verbs where the action was carried out on or by a 'self': **eu me levanto** *I get myself up*. You can also use reflexive verbs to convey a neutral verb subject, in the same way the French use 'on' (one). **Servem-se refeições** means *meals serve themselves*, i.e. *they are served*. This provides an alternative to saying *we serve* (**servimos**). You may also come across such examples as:

vende-se *for sale*	**compra-se** *is bought*
fala-se *is spoken*	**faz-se** *is made*

Keep a look-out for further examples, especially on signs and in adverts. It is also common to see and hear these as **se vende, se compra**, etc.

Dialogue 2

Sylvia is on her way to look at the grand Opera House in Manaus. At reception she overhears a conversation.

Hóspede (*guest*)	Queria me queixar de algumas coisas de que não estou muito contente.
Recepcionista	Qual é o problema, senhor?
Hóspede	Em primeiro lugar, o ar-condicionado não está funcionando, e com este calor e tantos mosquitos que temos aqui, não agüento ficar no quarto como está agora. Também a torneira da pia não fecha e a água continua pingando toda a noite.
Recepcionista	Peço mil desculpas. Vou chamar alguém para vir ver o quarto já já. Está bem?

Hóspede	OK, mas também precisa trocar o travesseiro por que está sujo, e dar uma olhada às persianas que não abrem direitinho.
Recepcionista	Muito bem, senhor. O senhor quer ir jantar enquanto organizo tudo?

queixar-se de	*to complain about*
contente	*happy*
em primeiro lugar	*first of all*
o ar-condicionado	*air-conditioning*
não está funcionando	*isn't working*
mosquitos (os)	*mosquitoes*
como está agora	*as it is now*
torneira (a)	*tap*
pia (a)	*basin*
não fecha	*doesn't close*
continua pingando	*carries on dripping*
peço mil desculpas	*I'm very sorry*
alguém	*someone*
já já	*right away*
travesseiro (o)	*pillow*
sujo	*dirty*
dar uma olhada	*to have a look*
persianas (as)	*blinds*
direitinho	*properly*
enquanto	*whilst*
organizo	*I organize*

Exercise 2

Name three things wrong with the guest's room.

1
2
3

Grammar

Making complaints

In a country as huge as Brazil, it is unfortunately inevitable that something will go wrong at some point. Look at the following check-list of useful expressions:

o aquecimento *heating*
a luz *electricity*
a água *water*
o ar-condicionado *air conditioning* não funciona/
o chuveiro *shower* não está funcionando
a fechadura *lock* *doesn't work/*
isn't working

a toalha *towel* sujo *dirty*
os copos *glasses* está/ estão *is / are* partido *broken*
o garfo *fork* lascado *chipped*
a faca *knife*
a colher *spoon*
o prato *plate* falta / faltam *is / are missing*

Remember to make the verbs and adjectives agree with the noun, e.g.

as toalhas estão suj*as* *the towels are dirty*
falta*m* os copos *the glasses are missing / there aren't any glasses*

Remember to complain politely! Use **desculpe** to start with, and expressions such as:

pode vir ver	*can you come and look*
pode ajudar	*can you help*
é capaz de	*are you able to*
é possível	*is it possible*

Summary

tem um apartamento livre?	*do you have a room free?*
simples/duplo	*single/double*
com/sem banheiro/ café da manhã	*with/without bathroom/ breakfast*
para ... dias/pessoas	*for ... days/people*
fica no ... andar	*it's on the ... floor*
queria me queixar de ...	*I'd like to complain about ...*
o/a ... não está funcionando	*the ... isn't working*
falta/m ...	*there's a/some ... missing*
pode dar uma olhada/ ajudar/vir?	*can you have a look/help/come?*
peço mil desculpas	*I'm really sorry*

i **Apartamento** is the term used in Brazil for an *en-suite room*, otherwise **um quarto** (*room only*) is asked for. Hotels have a different star-rating from what you may have been used to, but you should be able to find something to suit your budget. A **pousada**, unlike in Portugal, is a B&B, although some may be quite pricey. Usually breakfast is included in the price of the room, and certainly worth having – normally a selection of ham, cheese, fruit, cakes and bread rolls. There is a good Youth Hostel service in many parts of Brazil (os **albergues de juventude**), and many motels are also worth considering – however you may be the only ones to still be there in the morning! If you can stand the comings and goings, these are really not a bad deal.

Practice

1 ▶ Take part in a dialogue on the tape about booking a room. Follow the pictures below for your prompts.

2 Match up the signs with the pictures.

i	ii	iii	iv	v
VENDE-SE	FAZEM-SE	COMPRAM-SE	FALA-SE	SERVEM-SE

3 ▶ Listen to someone booking into a hotel and fill in their details on the **ficha** below.

> Room type -
>
> With/without bathroom - - - - - - - - - - - - - - - - - -
>
> No. days -
>
> Departure day -
>
> Room No. -
>
> Price per night -

---

1 What complaint might you give in each of the following situations? Start with **Desculpe, ...**

   a a dirty fork
   b air conditioning not working
   c dripping tap
   d broken plate
   e spoon missing

5 Choose an appropriate verb from the box to complete the sentences.

   a Antes de _____ à cidade, vou ver minha amiga.
   b Và ao seu quarto sem _____ o jantar!
   c Ana vai viajar depois de _____ o trabalho.
   d O senhor quer sentar antes de _____ o filme?
   e Em vez de _____ água, vou tomar um chá.

ir	terminar	comer	ver	beber

Do you understand?

Look at the information taken as a room booking at the Hotel Ipanema, and answer the questions which follow it.

HOTEL IPANEMA INFORMAÇÃO TURÍSTICA

Nome
Roberto

Sobrenome
Silvini

Endereço
Via Romani, 45, Napoli

Nacionalidade
Italiano

Idade
38 anos

No. telefone
5-867 – 268 – 9961

Pagamento
Cartão crédito

Número de crianças, com
idades /   /   /

Tipo de alojamento
*Apartamento c/pensão
completa*

Quantos quartos?
*Um apt. duplo – cama de
casal*

Refeições:
Café / jantar

Quantas noites?
6

Extra no quarto:
TV / geladeira

Data da estadia:
Do 5 ao 11 de janeiro

---

1 Where does the client live?
2 How is he going to pay for the room?
3 How many rooms does he want?
4 Apart from a TV, what else does he want in the room?
5 What is the client's surname?
6 How old is he?
7 How many children will be coming?
8 Which meals does he want?

11

que tal esta?
what about this one?

In this unit you will learn
- how to further discuss likes and dislikes
- how to express preference
- how to shop for souvenirs
- how to buy snacks

▶ Dialogue 1

Before she leaves Amazônia, Sylvia visits a craft shop to buy some souvenirs.

Sylvia	Bom dia. Estou procurando presentes para minha família. Tem alguma coisa típica do Brasil?
Vendedora	Temos lembranças muito bonitas aqui – típicas da região, e todas feitas a mão. O artesanato aqui é indígeno, feito pelas tribos do Amazonas.
Sylvia	Quanto custa esta bolsa?
Vendedora	Esta é de couro e custa 24 reais. Gosta?
Sylvia	Sim, adoro, mas tem uma menor? É para minha irmã e ela prefere uma bolsa pequena.
Vendedora	Que tal esta? Também é bonita. Ou tem este chaveiro.
Sylvia	Prefiro a bolsa. Agora, que tem para homens?
Vendedora	Temos cachimbos, carteiras, botas, bengalas …
Sylvia	Bom, meu marido detesta fumar, então não vale a pena levar cachimbo. Acho que ele vai ficar encantado com uma bengala.
Vendedora	E para si?
Sylvia	Mm, para mim, bem, eu gosto muito de brincos. Tem?
Vendedora	Temos estes feitos de plantas e de plumas – uma recordação linda desta magnífica parte do mundo.
Sylvia	Tem razão. Então levo os brincos, a bolsa e a bengala. Obrigada.

estou procurando	*I'm looking for*
presente (o)	*gift*
lembranças (as)	*souvenirs*
região (a)	*region*
feitas a mão	*hand-made*
artesanato (o)	*handicrafts*
indígeno	*indigenous*
tribo (a)	*tribe*
o Amazonas	*Amazon*
que tal esta?	*what about this one?*
chaveiro (o)	*key-ring*
para homens	*for men*
cachimbo (o)	*pipe*
carteiras (as)	*purses/wallets*
bengalas (as)	*walking sticks*

fumar	*to smoke*
não vale a pena	*it's not worth it*
encantado	*very happy*
brincos (os)	*earrings*
feitos de plantas/plumas	*made of plants/feathers*
recordação (a)	*reminder*
esta magnífica parte	*this magnificent part of*
do mundo	*the world*

Grammar

Likes, dislikes

In Unit 6 you learnt how to use verbs of liking, disliking and preferring, when talking about your favourite leisure activities. In this dialogue you can see how the same verbs are used when referring to objects: **Ela prefere uma bolsa pequena** *she prefers a small ba*g. Be careful with the spelling of **odiar** *to hate*: **odeio/odeia/ odiamos/odeiam;** and don't forget **preferir** – **prefiro/prefere/preferimos/preferem.**

Para você For you

When using the preposition **para** (*for*) with pronouns, you should use the following:

	mim *me*		**nos** *us*
	ele *him*		**eles** *them*
para *for*	**ela** *her*		**elas** *them*
	si *himself/herself/yourself*		**si** *themselves/yourselves*
	você *you*		**vocês** *you*

These forms are also used with other prepositions. Look at these examples:

Eu gosto de fazer coisas para eles.	*I like doing things for them.*
Elas fazem tudo para si.	*They do everything for themselves.*
João pensa sempre em mim.	*John always thinks about me.*

Lembranças do Brasil Souvenirs from Brazil

As you travel around Brazil you will come across varied and exquisite souvenirs. Here are a few suggestions for what to buy:

gaucho-style tea and drinking vessel	chá erva mate (chimarrão) e cuia (cambuca)
precious rocks	pedras preciosas
gold	ouro
diamond	diamante
leather goods	artigos de couro
earthenware pottery	cerâmica de barra
wall hangings	tapeçarias
hammocks	redes

Souvenir expressions

Revise shopping expressions, such as:

posso ver/experimentar
gosto mais deste/daquele
tem outro/menor/maior
tem em + *colour*
de que é feito?

Dialogue 2

Sylvia meets a friend for a quick snack before getting ready to leave for Brasília.

Sylvia Oi, Paulo. Tudo bem?

Paulo Tudo, e você?

Sylvia Ótimo. Esta viagem é muito interessante para mim. Amanhã parto para Brasília.

Paulo Vai achar Brasília super-diferente – moderna, a sede do governo.

Garçom Que vão tomar?

Sylvia Para mim um café com leite e um lanche.

Garçom De que? Temos hamburguer, cheeseburguer-maionese, coxinhas e empadas.

Sylvia Ai, que difícil! Acho que quero uma empada. Paulo, o que você vai pedir?

Paulo Para mim, um suco de maracujá, uma coxinha, e um sanduíche de queijo.

esta viagem	this journey	um lanche	snack
parto para	I leave for	que difícil!	how difficult!
vai achar	you'll find	super-diferente	really different
a sede do governo	the seat of government		

i Snacks and drinks in Brazilian cafés

Bebidas *Drinks*

frias	cold	quentes	hot
guaraná	national soft drink	chá	tea
vitamina	milk shake	café	coffee
leite	milk	média	milky coffee
suco de fruta	fruit juice		
chope	draft lager		
laranjada	orangeade		

Lanches *Snacks*

bolo	cake
sanduíche de – presunto/queijo	ham/cheese sandwich
torrada com manteiga	toast with butter
coxinha	chicken 'drumstick'
empada	pie
cheeseburguer/maionese	cheeseburger/mayonnaise

Summary

estou procurando presentes para ...	*I'm looking for presents for ...*
tem alguma coisa típica?	*do you have anything typical?*
que tal este/esta?	*what about this?*
que tem para ...?	*what do you have for ...?*
levo ...	*I'll take ...*
para mim, para meu irmão	*for me, for my brother*
o que vai pedir?	*what are you going to have?*
um sanduíche de queijo/presunto	*a cheese/ham sandwich*
quero um lanche	*I want a snack*

Practice

1 Complete the sentences by using the correct form of a verb of liking/disliking, plus the appropriate name for the souvenir in the picture.

a Ela (odiar) a _____.

b Eu (não gostar) dos
   _____.

c Nós (preferir) _____ a
   _____.

d Você (gostar) dos _____?

e Eles (adorar) os _____.

2 Choose the correct pronouns out of those given.

a Este bolo é para **me/mim**.
b Joana não gosta **deles/dos**.
c Você pensa **nela/na**?
d Fazem o trabalho para **se/si**.
e O livro é para **você/o**.

3 Read each person's snack preferences, then choose what each would have.

a Sarah wants a hot drink without milk — 1 cafezinho 2 média

b Tony is vegetarian — 1 sanduíche de presunto 2 torrada

c Sally prefers sweet things — 1 bolo 2 coxinha 3 empada

d David wants an alcoholic drink — 1 suco 2 chope 3 chá

e Mary hates soft drinks — 1 guaraná 2 leite 3 laranjada

4 ▶ Take part in a dialogue on the tape, where you are buying souvenirs for your family.

You	(Say *I'm looking for presents for my family*)
Sra	Temos umas coisas bonitas e típicas do Brasil.
You	(Say *do you have a hammock?*)
Sra	Temos estas, que são bonitas.
You	(Ask *how much it is*)
Sra	Esta custa 156 reais.
You	(Say *what do you have for ladies*)
Sra	Para senhoras temos tapeçarias, pedras, artigos de couro ...
You	(Say *I'm going to take the hammock, and this wall hanging*)
Sra	Obrigada.

Do you understand?

Mônica is a 'national heroine' in Brazilian cartoon strips. How much of the text below can you understand?

1 In how many countries has Mônica already made her presence felt?
2 When is she going to be launched elsewhere?
3 In how many other countries?
4 In the US marketplace, where will Mônica have to be seen to be attending?
5 In Brazil, what else is the Sousa Production Company launching?
6 What do you think are the words for:
  a little rabbit b cartoons c classes

Mônica vai às aulas

Com o coelhinho na mão, a personagem Mônica ataca outra vez. Presente timidamente em dezessete países, a partir do ano que vem a heroína dos quadrinhos de Maurício de Sousa vai penetrar com força total em quarenta outros, começando pelos Estados Unidos. Para entrar no mercado americano, Mônica terá de freqüentar uma escola. Lá, não se admite faltar às aulas nem nas histórias em quadrinhos. No front interno, a Maurício de Sousa Produções lança o guaraná da Mônica e outros refrigerantes.

12 por que não vamos ao teatro?

why don't we go to the theatre?

In this unit you will learn
- how to plan an evening out
- how to get tickets for entertainment
- how to make an invitation
- more about time

▶ Dialogue 1

Whilst Sylvia is in Brasília she meets up with an old friend, Luciane. They are trying to decide what to do later that day.

Luciane Que quer fazer mais tarde?
Sylvia Não me importo. Decida você.
Luciane Que tal o cinema?
Sylvia Se quiser. Que filme está passando?
Luciane Deixe-me ver no jornal. Dê-me aqui. Bom, página 16, aqui está – guia de espetáculos vida noturna. Hmm, no cinema Tivoli está passando 'JFK', no ABC está passando 'Aliens', e no Brasilense 'Wall Street'.
Sylvia Ai, Lû, você sabe que não gosto nada destes tipos de filmes.
Luciane Então, fazer o quê?
Sylvia Por que não vamos ao teatro? Veja o que está passando.
Luciane Bem, tem uma peça satírica no teatro Marlsol – é sobre a política no Brasil de hoje em dia. Parece bem recebida pelo público.
Sylvia Ótimo. Vamos lá. A que horas começa?
Luciane Há uma sessão matiné às 3.15 da tarde, e a sessão da noite começa às 7.30. Que horas são agora?
Sylvia São 2.20. Ainda dá tempo para chegar. Vamos de táxi, é mais rápido. Vamos!

mais tarde	*later*
não me importo	*I'm not bothered*
decida você	*you decide*
se quiser	*if you like/want*
filme (o)	*film*
deixe-me ver	*let me see*
guia (o)	*guide*
página (a)	*page*
não gosto nada de	*I don't like at all*
fazer o quê?	*do what?*
veja	*see!*
peça (a)	*play*
satírica	*satirical*
sobre	*about*
política (a)	*politics*
hoje em dia	*nowadays*
parece bem recebida	*it seems well received*

público (o)	*public*
a que horas começa?	*what time does it start?*
a sessão matiné	*matinee*
ainda dá tempo	*there's still time*
rápido	*quick*
vamos!	*let's go*

Exercise

Can you answer these questions in Portuguese based on the dialogue?

a Qual é o filme no cinema ABC? _____
b Os filmes são brasileiros? _____
c Que tipo de peça há no teatro Marisol? _____
d Lû e Sylvia vão à sessão da tarde ou da noite? _____
e Que tipo de transporte elas vão usar? _____

Grammar

Dê-me aqui – more object pronouns

In the expression **dê-me**, what you are actually saying in Portuguese is *give to me*. In order to say *to me, to you*, etc. you need, unfortunately, another set of object pronouns, called indirect object pronouns. They are:

me	*to me*	**nos**	*to us*
lhe*	*to him/her/you*	**lhes**	*to them/you*

***te** (*to you*) is used more frequently than **lhe**.

You use these each time the English has the word *to* in front of the pronoun. You have to be on the look-out, though, because often this is omitted in English. Study this sentence:

Give him the book.

If we break it down, we have:

verb	**indirect object (pronoun)**	**direct object (noun)**
give	TO him	the book

In Portuguese this would then be: **lhe dê o livro** (or **dê-lhe o livro**).

You will also hear **dê o livro para ele**. This is often the case in colloquial speech.

Pronouns galore!

So far you have met quite a variety of these types of words, and as many people find these small expressions confusing, let's compare them all in a table to help you recognize and learn them.

subject	direct object	indirect object	reflexive
eu	me	me	me
você ele ela	o, a	lhe	se
nós	nos	nos	nos
vocês eles elas	os, as	lhes	se

Changes following verbs

With direct object pronouns in the third person (o, a, os, as), certain changes occur after verbs which help pronunciation. These changes take place in the following situations:

a Following verb forms ending in -r, -s, and -z

These final letters are omitted, and an -l is added to the beginning of the pronoun. In the case of the omission of final -r, the following written accents are added to the remaining final vowel of the verb.

> -ar verbs: -á
> -er verbs: -ê
> -ir verbs: -i (no accent)

> **Vou vender meu carro**   *I'm going to sell my car*
> **Vou vendê-lo**   *I'm going to sell it*

b Following verb forms ending in -m, -ão, and -õe (nasal sounds)

The endings are maintained, but an **n** is added before the pronoun to preserve the nasal sound.

> **Eles fazem o bolo**   *They make the cake*
> **Eles fazem-no**   *They make it*

Remember that in standard Portuguese usage, object pronouns *usually* follow the verb. However, Brazilian usage is more fluid, and in the spoken language particularly, you will find the pronouns before the verb in many instances.

To accent or not to accent?

It can be confusing to come across similar words with the addition, or absence, of written accents, as in the following. This is what they mean:

> (o) que(?) = *that, which, what(?)*
> (o) quê? = *what?* (used on its own)
> por quê? = *why?* used on its own, or at end of sentence
> porque = *because*
> por que ...? = *why ...?*

Look at these examples:

> Gosto muito de café. Por quê? Porque é muito saboroso.
> O que você vai comprar? Um avião. O quê?
> Por que não vai ao cinema? Porque é tarde.
> O cinema que eu prefiro é perto de minha casa.

Making suggestions

You can use the following expressions:

Que tal ...?	*What about ...?*
Que tal o teatro?	*What about the theatre?*
Que tal a gente* ir ao museu?	*What about us going to the museum?*

***a gente** = colloq. *us*

Por que não vai/vamos ...?	*Why don't you/we go ...?*
Que prefere fazer?	*What do you prefer to do?*
Que quer fazer?	*What do you want to do?*
Vamos ...?	*Let's/shall we ...?*

Possible replies might include:

ótimo	*great*	**prefiro/preferia**	*I prefer/would prefer*
está bem	*OK*	**quero/queria**	*I want/would like*
OK	*OK*	**boa idéia**	*good idea*
não estou a fim de ...	*I don't feel like ...*		

Describing events

Here are some positive and negative adjectives you may want to use to talk about the cinema, theatre, etc.

É um filme *film*
uma peça *play*
um concerto *concert*
uma coleção *collection*
uma exposição *exhibition*
um show *show*

romântico *romantic*
satírico *satirical*
cômico *comical*
triste *sad*
dramático *dramatic*
interessante *interesting*
chato *boring*
fascinante *fascinating*
crítico *critical*

Starting/finishing times

The rules you learnt for time in Unit 5 apply to the starting and finishing times of events:

A que horas começa?	*What time does it begin?*
Começa às ...	*It begins at ...*
A que horas termina?	*What time does it finish?*
Termina às ...	*It finishes at ...*
Há um intervalo { das ... às ...	*There is an interval { from ... to ...*
{ de 15 minutos	*{ of 15 minutes*

▶ Dialogue 2

After the play, Sylvia and Lû decide on the rest of the evening.

Sylvia Que boa peça! Foi ótima. Só que não entendi tudo.

Lû Às vezes é difícil – você precisa saber tudo sobre os políticos e a corrupção neste país. Mas gostei.

Sylvia E agora, Lû. Que fazemos? Voltamos a pé ou apanhamos um táxi?

Lû Por que não tomamos um copo ali naquele barzinho, e depois vamos jantar naquele restaurante de que você gosta?

Sylvia Mas preciso me preparar para amanhã – vou viajar por Goiânia.

Lû Venha, eu te convido, e sou eu quem paga.

Sylvia Ai, isso não, a gente divide.

Lû Não, insisto. Você é minha convidada aqui e hóspede neste país. Pago eu.

Sylvia Está bem. Aceito. E você pode me falar acerca do estado de Goiânia.

foi	*it was*
só que	*only/just that*
não entendi	*I didn't understand*
tudo	*everything*
políticos (os)	*politicians*
corrupção (a)	*corruption*
gostei	*I enjoyed (it)*
que fazemos?	*what shall we do?*
tomamos um copo	*let's have something to drink*
barzinho (o)	*small bar*
preparar	*to prepare*
venha	*come on!*
eu te convido	*I'll treat you*
sou eu quem pago	*I'll pay*
isso não	*no/oh, no*
a gente divide	*we'll split it*
insisto	*I insist*
convidada	*guest* (invited)
hóspede (o, a)	*guest*
pago eu!	*I'll pay*
aceito	*I accept*
acerca de	*about*
estado (o)	*state*

Grammar

Talking about the past

In the dialogue you were introduced very briefly to ways of talking about the past in Portuguese.

foi *it was*   **não entendi** *I didn't understand*   **gostei** *I liked*

You will learn the full formations and explanations in Unit 15.

Barzinho Little bar

One way of making things smaller, cuter, more affectionate in Portuguese is to add **-zinho** (or **-inho**) to the ending of the word in question. Hence:

o bar → o barzinho	*little bar*
o café → o cafezinho	*little coffee*
o livro → o livrinho	*little book/pamphlet*
o gato → o gatinho	*kitten*
obrigado → obrigadinho	*thanks very much*

Particular means of transport

When specifying a particular vehicle, e.g. a friend's car, or a timetabled bus/train, etc. you use **em (no/na)** and the vehicle, and not **de**. For example:

Vou *no* carro de José.   *I'm going in José's car.*
Ele vai *no* avião da Varig.   *He's going on the Varig plane.*
Vamos *no* trem das 2.30.   *We're going on the 2.30 train.*

Summary

que quer fazer mais tarde?	*what do you want to do later?*
que tal o cinema/o teatro?	*how about the cinema/theatre?*
não me importo	*I don't mind*
se quiser	*if you like/want*
por que não vamos ao museu?	*why don't we go to the museum?*
ainda dá tempo para ...	*there's still time to ...*
há um filme/uma peça/um show	*there's a film/play/show*
eu te convido	*it's my turn to pay for you (I invite you)*
sou eu quem pago/pago eu	*I'll pay*
você é meu/minha convidado/a	*you're my guest*

i Brazilians love enjoying themselves, and don't need a lot to make them happy. Even a drink in a bar can proceed into a table-patting, match-box shaking accompaniment of a song, and soon the whole place is alive with movement, rhythm and enjoyment. Larger towns and cities are blessed with museums, cinemas, theatres, nightclubs, galleries and plenty of places to eat, drink and soak up the atmosphere. For the more cultured visitor, there are concerts and literary events as well – just look in the local paper or ask at the **Turismo**.

If you don't fancy going out (although you'll miss Brazil if you don't), there are always the amazingly dramatic TV soap operas – the **tele-novelas**. Brazilians are hooked on them, some watching three, four or five of them daily! And we thought the Aussie soaps were abundant enough!

Practice

1 Can you do the following?

  a Suggest to a friend that you go to the museum.
  b Ask at what time the film starts.
  c Say the concert finishes at 10.30pm.
  d Say 'What a good exhibition'.
  e Tell John that he is your guest.
  f Say 'Shall we return by bus?'

2 Choose the correct pronouns from those given in the box, to fill the gaps.

  a _____ _____ levanto às sete horas.
  b Dá- _____ o bolo!
  c Não _____ importas?
  d _____ vai ao mercado.
  e Vou vendê- _____ à minha amiga.

me	ele	eu	te	lo	lhe

3 ▶ Listen to two people discussing how to spend the afternoon, and complete the exercise below by ticking the appropriate boxes, or filling in the missing information:

  a Marta suggests going to   i cinema   ii concert
  b What page is the info. on?   i 26   ii 23
  c What is Rui's preferred activity? i museum   ii cinema
  d What is on offer there?   _____
  e What time?   _____
  f How will they get there?   i bus   ii walk

4 Fill in your part of the dialogue, inviting a friend out.

  Friend E agora. Que fazemos?
  You   (Say *why don't we go and have lunch in that little bar over there?*)
  Friend Mas preciso me preparar para o trabalho.
  You   (Say *come along, I invite you and I'll pay.*)
  Friend Isso não.
  You   (Say *I insist – you are my guest.*)
  Friend Está bem. Aceito.
  You   (Say *let's go.*)

5 Fill in the gaps with a *preposition* [*prep.*] (**de/a/em**) or a *means of transport*, *location*, or *time*, according to the instructions. Don't forget the contracted forms **no**, **da**, **à** etc. – see Unit 2.

E.g.   *à*   *cidade*   *de* *ônibus*
     Vou [*prep.*] [THE TOWN] [*prep.*]

(*a*) Sónia vai viajar [*prep.*]   [*prep.*] Varig.

(*b*) Eles vão pegar o [*prep.*]   **14:00**

(*c*) Vamos [*prep.*] ? Não, prefiro ir [*prep.*]

(*d*) Quer vir [*prep.*] [*prep.*] meu pai?

Do you understand?

Read the three film excerpts below, and decide which title belongs with which film.

> i Brigada de Homicidis   ii Nascido a 4 de julho
>   iii Mulheres à beira de um ataque de nervos

Now answer the following:

a   Which film is not American?
b   Which film would you choose if you enjoy police stories?
c   Which war does film **c** relate to?
d   Is film **a** a comedy or tragedy?
c   How many people are killed in film **b**?
f   The adaptation for film **c** is taken from what source?

> **a**   Este é talvez o filme mais popular do mais consagrado cineasta espanhol: Pedro Almodóvar. Premiado em Berlim com os galardões destinados ao melhor realizador e à melhor atriz (Carmen Maura), o filme é, no fundo, uma grande tragédia, cujas situações levam o espectador a rir até às lágrimas.

b O detetive Robert Ross tenta incriminar um perigoso traficante de droga. Mas quando está prestes a deslindar o caso, é-lhe entregue o caso do assassínio de uma velha judia, cujo móbil terá o roubo. Por um lado, o assassínio da velha senhora desperta nele as velhas tradições a que nunca ligou. Por outro, o seu colega é morto, o que obriga Ross a dividir-se pelos dois casos.

c Nascido a 4 de julho de 1946, Ron Kovic oferece-se aos 20 anos como voluntário para o Vietname, desejoso de servir o seu país. Ferido em combate, torna-se paraplégico e herói nacional. Escreve as suas memórias e é esta autobiografia que Oliver Stone (*Platoon, Wall Street, JFK*) – também combatente no Vietname – adapta, num filme que recebe o Oscar de melhor realizador. Para o papel do protagonista, Stone escolheu, contra a opinião de muitos, Tom Cruise, e o jovem ator é na composição da figura de Kovic.

13 é tudo?
is that everything?

In this unit you will learn
- how to obtain postal services
- how to buy groceries
- how to deal with car hire, parking and petrol

▶ Dialogue 1

Sylvia has bought some postcards (**postais**), and goes to the post office (**correio**) to buy stamps.

Sylvia	Bom dia. Quanto custa enviar um postal para Inglaterra, por favor?
Empregada	2 reais e cinqüenta centavos.
Sylvia	E este pacote? Por via aérea?
Empregada	Ponha na balança. Agora, pesa um quilo e cem gramas, então custa 7 reais e noventa centavos.
Sylvia	Bom, então queria seis selos para postais, e quero enviar o pacote também.
Empregada	São 22 reais e noventa centavos no total.
Sylvia	Aqui tem uma nota de cinqüenta.
Empregada	(*counts change*) Agora dez centavos dá vinte e três, vinte e quatro, vinte e cinco, trinta, e vinte dá cinqüenta.
Sylvia	Obrigada. Onde é a caixa?
Empregada	É ali à direita; ponha no lado esquerdo, onde diz 'estrangeiro'.

enviar	*to send*	**pesa**	*It weighs*
postal(o)/postais	*postcard/s*	**quilo (o)**	*kilo*
pacote (o)	*parcel*	**gramas (os)**	*grammes*
por via aérea	*by air mail*	**no total**	*in all*
ponha	*put*	**caixa (a)**	*post box*
balança (a)	*scales*	**estrangeiro (o)**	*abroad*

▶ Dialogue 2

Next Sylvia goes to a local grocery store (a **mercearia** or **minimercado**) to buy some food for her few days away in the countryside.

Dono (*owner*)	Bom dia. Pois não?
Sylvia	Bom dia. Queria pão por favor. Tem pãezinhos?
Dono	Aqui. Quantos quer?
Sylvia	Meia dúzia. E um pacote de manteiga.
Dono	Que mais?
Sylvia	Tem presunto?
Dono	Temos este, que é muito bom, ou aquele (*pointing*), que também é saboroso.

Sylvia	Me dê 250 gramas deste aqui, por favor.
Dono	Mais alguma coisa?
Sylvia	Sim, tem um bom queijo?
Dono	Este queijo é excelente. Quer provar um pedaço deste?
Sylvia	Mmm, que delícia. Me corte meio quilo por favor.
Dono	É tudo?
Sylvia	Só faltam umas garrafas de água, uma de guaraná, que adoro, e estas coisinhas que tenho aqui no carrinho.
Dono	Muito bem. São 36 reais no total. Obrigado e boa viagem.

pãezinhos (os)	bread rolls
quantos?	how many?
meia dúzia	half a dozen
pacote (o)	packet
excelente	excellent
pedaço (o)	bit
é tudo?	is that everything?
só faltam	they're just missing/needed
que mais?	what else
saboroso	tasty
deste	of this
mais alguma coisa?	anything else?
provar	to taste
que delícia	delicious
me corte	cut me
garrafas (as)	bottles
coisinhas (as)	few things/little things
carrinho (o)	trolley

True or false?

Answer **verdadeiro** or **falso** to these statements.

		V	F
a	Sylvia quer comprar oito pãezinhos.		
b	O senhor não tem presunto.		
c	Sylvia prova um queijo antes de comprar.		
d	Sylvia compra uma garrafa de cerveja.		

Grammar

Quantities for shopping

Weights and measures (metric, of course!)

1 k	**um quilo**	1 l	**um litro**
½ k	**meio quilo**	½ l	**meio litro**
250 g	**250 gramas**	250 dl	**um quarto de litro**
100 g	**100 gramas**		

Other quantities

um pacote	*packet*	**uma caixa**	*box*
um rolo	*roll*	**um tubo**	*tube*
uma barra	*bar*	**um frasco**	*jar*
uma lata	*tin, can*		

One of this, some of those

These expressions are often lifesavers when you do not know, or cannot remember, the names of items. You can simply point and say:

um/uma *one*
uns/umas *some*
um pouco *a little*

{
deste/desta *of this*
destes/destas *of these*
daquele/daquela *of that*
daqueles/daquelas *of those*

This here, that there

You have already learnt that **este** (**esta**) means *this* (*thing here*), and **aquele** (**aquela**), means *that* (*thing there*). There are also the words **esse, essa, esses, essas**, which refer to the thing nearest the person with whom you are talking.

a **esta flor aqui**
this flower here

b **essa flor aí (que você tem)**
that flower you have there

c **aquela flor ali**
that flower over there

Quanto? How much?

Quanto is used as an adjective in expressions such as **quantos quer?** (e.g. **quantos pãezinhos**). If you were buying bottles, you would be asked **quantas?** (**garrafas**). Used as a question (**quanto é?, quanto custa/m?, quanto vale?**) it doesn't change form.

Groceries

The following check list may be useful

os ovos	*eggs*	**os biscoitos**	*biscuits*
o queijo	*cheese*	**os cereais**	*cereals*
o mel	*honey*	**o azeite**	*olive oil*
a farinha	*flour*	**o açúcar**	*sugar*
o molho	*sauce*	**a massa**	*pasta*

Summary

Here is a summary of shopping expressions

Quanto custa?	*How much does it cost?*
Tem?	*Do you have?*
Quanto/a/os/as quer?	*How much/many do you want?*
Que mais?	*What else?*
Me dê/corte (Dê-me) ...	*Give/cut me ...*
Mais alguma coisa?	*Anything else?*
É tudo?	*Is that all?*
Pois não?	*Can I help you?*
São ... no total	*That's ... in all.*
Este, esse, aquele	*this, that, that*

i Post offices usually open from 9 till 6 during the week, although some close for lunch. Postage is expensive in general, as is faxing. The queues are enough to try the patience of a saint, but in larger branches you can now buy stamps at the philatelic desk. You can recognize the Post Office by the ECT sign – **Empresa de Correios e Telégrafos**.

Shops also open at the above times, with the smaller ones closing for lunch (between 11.30am and 2pm). On Saturdays shops tend to close at lunchtimes, apart from the larger shopping centres and supermarkets.

Practice

1 Fill in your part of this dialogue in a post office.

You	(Say *good afternoon; how much does it cost to send this parcel to Germany, please?*).
Empregada	Ponha na balança. Agora, dois quilos, então são 13 reais.
You	(Say *right, I'd like to send the parcel, and I would also like 10 stamps*)
Empregada	Para a Alemanha também?
You	(Say *no, 3 for Spain and 7 for England*)
Empregada	São 35 reais e setenta centavos.
You	(Say *thank you; where is the post box?*)
Empregada	É ali, à esquerda.

2 ▶ Look at Miguel's shopping list below, and then listen to his conversation at the **minimercado**. Tick off everything he buys, put a cross by what is not available, and write down in English the extra item he buys.

> ½ *dúzia de ovos*
>
> *açúcar*
>
> *2 pacotes biscoitos*
>
> *frasco de mel*
>
> *presunto —*
> *250 gramas*
>
> *1½ litros cerveja*
>
> *8 pãezinhos*

Extra item = _____

3 Fill in the gaps using the appropriate form of **este, esse** or **aquele**.

a _____ postal aqui é para minha amiga.
b Qual manteiga? _____ que você tem aí.
c _____ senhores ali são italianos.
d _____ pãezinhos aqui são muito bons.
e _____ balas que você tem são deliciosas.

4 ▶ Grocery bingo. Here is your Bingo card, containing five items of grocery. Listen to the voice on the tape, who will call out various items, and cross off those on your card when you hear them. When you've heard all five, shout Bingo! If you have done so correctly, you should hear the voice congratulate you (**parabéns**).

▶ Dialogue 3

Sylvia goes to a car-hire agency.

Sylvia Boa tarde. Eu posso alugar um carro aqui?
Empregado Claro. Tem todos os documentos necessários?
Sylvia Aqui, tome.
Empregado Bom, estão todos em ordem. Agora, é para quantos dias?
Sylvia Para quatro, começando de hoje. Tem algo econômico, mas ao mesmo tempo confortável? Quero ver um pouco da região.
Empregado Temos um Ford, que custa 53 reais por dia, mais 6 por quilômetro. O preço inclui o seguro.

| | Sylvia | Ótimo! |
| Empregado | Agora, é só assinar aqui e aqui, e pronto. Não se esqueça de trazer o carro de volta com o tanque cheio. |

alugar	to hire, rent	**inclui**	includes
necessários	necessary	**seguro (o)**	insurance
em ordem	in order	**não se esqueça**	don't forget
começando	beginning	**de volta**	back
econômico	reasonable	**o tanque**	tank
ao mesmo tempo	at the same time	**cheio**	full (filled)

▶ Dialogue 4

Whilst she is looking at a map, Sylvia is approached by a policeman (**um policial**).

Policial Boa tarde. Sabe que é proibido estacionar aqui?

Sylvia Ah, boa tarde, senhor policial. Ainda bem que está aqui. Parece que estou perdida. O que faço para chegar em Goiânia?

Policial Goiânia é? Bom, o melhor é virar aqui para a esquerda, tomar aquela estrada, e continuar até ao próximo cruzamento. Depois vai ver os sinais.

proibido	prohibited	**estrada (a)**	main road
estacionar	to park	**cruzamento (o)**	crossroads
ainda bem	thank goodness	**sinais (os)**	traffic signs
o melhor é	the best thing to do is	**perdida**	lost

▶ Dialogue 5

Later Sylvia stops for petrol.

Sylvia Boa tarde. Ponha 15 litros por favor.

Empregado De normal, sem chumbo, gasóleo ou de álcool?

Sylvia Creio que é sem chumbo. É carro alugado.

Empregado Ah sim; olhe, aqui diz sem chumbo. Então 15 litros. É tudo?

Sylvia É possível verificar a água e o óleo para mim?

Empregado Claro. Um momento só. Está tudo OK.

Sylvia Obrigada.

normal	2-star petrol	alugado	hired
gasóleo	diesel	olhe	look
sem chumbo	unleaded	aqui diz	here it says
álcool	alcohol	verificar	to check
	(used in Brazil)	óleo (o)	oil

Grammar

Por For, per, through

The preposition **por** *for* is used in expressions with prices, e.g. **reais por dia** *reais per day*. **Por** contracts into **pelo, pela, pelos** and **pelas** when combined with the article, e.g. **vou pela cidade** = *I'm going through (by) the town*.

Verbs as adjectives

Estou perdida/carro alugado, are examples of verbs used as adjectives, what is called the 'past participle'. This is the part in English such as 'seen, broken, parked, opened', etc. In Portuguese, it is formed in the following way:

	remove infinitive ending	add past participle ending	past participle
falar *to speak*	-ar	-ado	**falado** *spoken*
comer *to eat*	-er	-ido	**comido** *eaten*
partir *to depart/ leave/break*	-ir	-ido	**partido** *departed/ left/broken*

Be careful with irregular verbs. Here are some examples:

ver → visto   vir → vindo
fazer → feito   abrir → aberto
escrever → escrito   pagar → pago

Rules of adjectives then apply. For example:

A casa é feita de madeira.   *The house is made of wood.*
As janelas estão partidas.   *The windows are broken.*

You will come across past participles again, in use as part of a past tense in Portuguese.

O melhor é ... **The best thing to do is ...**

This construction can be used with a variety of adjectives as well as with **melhor** (*best*).

O importante é ...	*The important thing is ...*
O pior é ...	*The worst thing is ...*
O triste é ...	*The sad thing is ...*

i **Petrol**: sugar cane alcohol is the normal fuel, although diesel is also very common. Many roads are terrible, some not more than dirt tracks. You may well need a credit card to hire a car, unless you have **reais** in cash. Insurance in Brazil may not give you full cover, so do be aware of what you are signing for.

Practice

5 Now see if you can do the following:

a Ask if you can rent a car here.
b Say it's for 8 days, starting today.
c Ask what you do to get to Rio.
d Say 'I seem to be lost'.
e Say 'Put in 12 litres of alcohol, please'.
f Ask 'Can you check the water for me?'

6 Choose an appropriate past participle for each sentence from the box and make any necessary alterations to it to use it as an adjective.

a O banco está _____.
b Todas as janelas estão _____.
c Os sapatos são _____ de couro.
d A conta já está _____.
e A carta está _____, senhor Mendes.

aberto	pago	feito	fechado	escrito

7 ▶ Listen to someone at a petrol station and indicate on the grid the services they require. [Recording activity 3]

Petrol – tick which type	How much?	Check water/oil	Price
Alcohol/Unleaded/Diesel			

8 **Estou perdido ...** Fill in the gaps in this dialogue: replace the English words by Portuguese ones.

Policial (*Good morning*) _____ _____. É (*prohibited*) _____ estacionar aqui nesta (*town square*) _____.

Sra. Desculpe. Acho que estou (*lost*) _____. O que faço para chegar no (*Rio*) _____?

Policial Bom, o melhor é virar aqui para a (*right*) _____, seguir até aos (*signs*) _____, e depois tomar a (*2nd*) _____ à (*left*) _____, e continuar naquela (*main road*) _____.

Do you understand?

Can you link up the roadsigns with their corresponding instructions?

a   i   área escolar

b   ii   aeroporto

c   iii   vento lateral

d   iv   cuidado, animais

e   v   semáforo à frente

f   vi   siga em frente

g   vii   vira à direita

h   viii   proibido virar à esquerda

i   ix   proibido trânsito de bicicletas

j   x   siga em frente ou à esquerda

k   xi   velocidade máxima permitida

l   xii   pedestre ande pela esquerda

14

está livre amanhã de tarde?

are you free tomorrow afternoon?

In this unit you will learn
- how to make plans for the future
- how to make arrangements to meet people
- how to deal with a telephone call
- the months of the year

▶ Dialogue 1

Sylvia overhears two people discussing their week-end plans whilst she is in a café in Campinas.

Moço (*Boy*)	Que vai fazer sábado de manhã, Teresa?
Moça (*Girl*)	Gostaria de fazer aquela viagem para o Pantanal, já que temos férias neste momento. Quer vir comigo?
Moço	Eu quero, sim. Ouvi dizer que é uma viagem fantástica, a gente viaja no trem da morte, há-de ser super-legal.
Moça	Não posso esperar – sempre quis ir. Sabe que a gente pode ver animais – há jacaré e tudo. Vamos até a Bolívia e depois voltamos. Leva mais ou menos uma semana para ir e voltar.
Moço	Ótimo. Olhe, eu aos sábados, costumo ir ao mercado bem cedo com minha mãe, mas estou livre a partir das oito e meia. Onde nos vamos encontrar?
Moça	Na Rodoviária. Temos que ir primeiro a Sampa para apanhar o trem. Eu estarei lá às nove horas. Tá?
Moço	Tá bem. A gente se vê no sábado. Tchau.
Moça	Tchau. E não se esqueça da máquina fotográfica, tá?

gostaria de	*I would like to*
o Pantanal	*swamp area near Bolivia*
já que	*seeing as*
férias (as)	*holidays*
neste momento	*at the moment*
ouvi dizer que	*I heard that*
a gente = nós	*we*
viaja	*travel*
há-de ser	*it's bound to be*
super-legal	*brilliant, cool*
esperar	*to wait*
sempre quis ir	*I've always wanted to go*
animais (os)	*animals*
jacaré (o)	*alligator*
leva	*it takes*
costumo	*I usually*
bem cedo	*really early*
a partir das	*from*
encontrar	*to meet*
temos que ir	*we have to go*
Sampa	*São Paulo*
estarei	*I will be*
tá = está?	*OK*
a gente se vê	*we'll see each other*
máquina fotográfica (a)	*camera*

▶ Dialogue 2

Back in her hotel, Sylvia has a call from a university aquaintance.

Sylvia	Alô?
Nelson	Alô, Sylvia?
Sylvia	Sim, quem fala?
Nelson	Daqui fala Nelson Gusmão, da Unicamp.
Sylvia	Oi, Nelson, tudo bem?
Nelson	Eu estou muito bem. E você?
Sylvia	Tudo azul. Como sabia meu número?
Nelson	Foi o José que me disse. Então, como vai sua grande 'tour' do Brasil?
Sylvia	Estou adorando. Estou fazendo boas amizades e desfrutando do tempo para explorar o país.
Nelson	Bom, você esta livre amanhã de tarde?
Sylvia	Estou, sim. Tenho que fazer um trabalho até ao meio-dia, mas depois estou livre. Por quê?
Nelson	Por que não vamos jogar tênis?
Sylvia	Está bem. A que horas nos encontramos?
Nelson	Às 2.30. Passo pelo hotel para te pegar. OK?
Sylvia	OK. Até amanhã.
Nelson	Tchau. Até amanhã.

alô	*hello* (on phone)
daqui fala	*this is*
Unicamp	*University in Campinas*
tudo azul	*everything just fine*
tempo (o)	*the time*
explorar	*to explore*
sabia	*you knew*
disse	*told*
amizades (as)	*friendships*
desfrutando	*taking advantage (of)*
passo	*I'll pass*
pelo hotel	*by the hotel*

Grammar

Future plans: *ir* + verbs

The easiest and most common way of talking about future actions is to use the verb **ir** *to go* plus the infinitive of any verb.

We do the same in English – *I'm going to visit Italy next summer./We're going to buy a car next week.*

Remind yourself of the formation of **ir** from Unit 3.

Vou visitar minha tia na semana que vem.	*I'm going to visit my aunt next week.*
Jaime vai comprar um livro amanhã.	*James is going to buy a book tomorrow.*
Vamos ganhar na loteria no sábado.	*We're going to win the lottery on Saturday.*

Future plans: future tense

You can also use the future tense, of course, to discuss your future actions, although in practice it is used less in spoken Portuguese. It can be used to emphasize particularly important actions. It is formed in the following way:

To the inifinitive of any verb add:	-ei	-emos
	-á	-ão

e.g.	**comprarei**	*I shall buy*
	falarão	*they/you* (pl.) *will talk*

However, there are three exceptions:

fazer = **far** + endings
trazer = **trar** + endings
dizer = **dir** + endings

All other verbs follow the regular pattern – a welcome relief to all learners! In Dialogue 1, the girl said **estarei lá** – *I shall be there*. She could also have said **vou estar lá,** and even just **estou lá.** In colloquial Portuguese, it is common to substitute the present tense for the future.

e.g.	**Compro um carro amanhã.**	*I'll buy a car tomorrow.*
	Te vejo no domingo.	*See you on Sunday.*

Future plans: future times

You will need some time phrases to express your future actions.

amanhã	*tomorrow*
depois de amanhã	*the day after tomorrow*
a semana/o mês/o ano que vem	*next week/month/year*
o/a próximo/a semana, mês, ano	*next week/month/year*
domingo/no sábado, etc.	*Sunday/on Saturday, etc.*

Gostaria I'd like

Gostaria is an example of a verb in what is termed a 'conditional' form. In English, we use the word *would* in conditionals. If you think that conditional actually means there is a 'condition' imposed on the action, it may help you to understand these structures. For example, *I would buy a car* (but I don't have the money). *If I had the money* is the condition. With the example of the verb *to like*, the condition may be seen in terms of *I would like to … if that's OK/if I may*. Conditionals do lead into a complex part of Portuguese verb usage; however the actual formation is as straightforward as that of the future tense.

Infinitive + -ia   -íamos
　　　　　　-ia   -iam

(**Fazer** becomes **faria**, **trazer** becomes **traria**, and **dizer** becomes **diria**.)

Eu compraria um carro.	*I would buy a car.*
Maria falaria com ele.	*Maria would speak with him.*

Obligation

In Portuguese there are various ways to express obligation or *having to do something*. The most commonly used in the spoken language is **ter que** or **ter de**, as in Sylvia's **tenho que fazer um trabalho** … In English we would say *I've got to* … Stronger obligation is expressed through the verb **dever** *to have to/must*. Here it is almost your duty to do something.

Devo terminar este trabalho `antes de sair.**	*I must finish this work before going out.*

And in expressions such as:

Eles devem estar perdidos.	*They must be lost.*

There is also the use of the verb **haver** *to have*, plus **de**, which conveys even stronger duty, something which is really bound to happen.

hei-de	hemos de
há-de	hão-de

For example:

Hei-de ganhar na loteria.   *I've just got to win the lottery.*
Há-de ser bom.   *It's bound to be good.*

It is also common to see these written without the hyphen, e.g. hei de ...

A partir de ... From ...

When you want to say 'from [a certain point] onwards' you use **a partir de** plus a point in time. This can be with the time: **a partir das duas horas** *from 2 o'clock*, or time phrases: **a partir de domingo** *from Sunday*; **a partir do mês que vem** *from next month*, etc.

The gerund: -ing

In Unit 6 you met this formation: **-ando/-endo/-indo**. Sylvia uses a few examples to talk about what she is currently involved in doing: **Estou adorando ..., fazendo ..., desfrutando ...**

With the verb **estar** in the present tense, this structure conveys an action currently taking place. For example:

Eles estão falando.   *They are talking (now).*
Agora estamos dormindo.   *Now we are sleeping.*
Eu estou aprendendo   *I am (currently) learning*
   português.   *Portuguese.*

i The **pantanal** is a great swampland area bordering the central-west part of Brazil and into Bolivia. The train crosses the middle of it and offers hardy travellers a marvellous panorama of its wildlife – alligators, birds, insects and big cats abound.

The **trem da morte**, or *train of death*, is the subject of many a traveller's tale – you need to watch your belongings, and be wary of people offering you food or drinks.

Telephone calling – in Rio, particularly, the telephone booths are called **orelhão** *big ear*, because of their design. In some you need to buy *discs* (**fichas**) in a local bar or kiosk, although phone cards are being introduced in many areas. The number 6 in phone numbers is referred to as **meia** (*half*) – from half a dozen.

Practice

1 Now see if you can do the following:

a Ask Paul what he's going to do on Wednesday afternoon.
b Say you'll be there at 10.30.
c Suggest to your friend that you go swimming.
d Ask someone what time you'll be meeting.
e Say you're free from 4.15 onwards.
f Answer the phone and ask who's calling.

2 ▶ Listen to this telephone conversation between two friends and answer the questions below.

a Who is calling?
b From where?
c When does he want to see his friend?
d What will Paulo be doing?
e What does Paulo's friend suggest?
f What time will he pick Paulo up?
g Where?

3 Make sentences by choosing words from each box, and forming the correct part of the future tense. A variety of answers may be correct. You will find samples in the Key.

	Time	Person	Action	End
a	amanhã	Cristina	visitar	um bolo
b	o mês que vem	eles	comprar	na loteria
c	no domingo	eu	escrever	Alemanha
d	o próximo ano	a Sra Lopes	ganhar	uma carta
e	depois de amanhã	nós	fazer	um carro

4 Decide what is currently going on in each picture, and write it down, forming the correct parts of estar and the gerund.

a Eles [estar] _____.
b A Sra [estar] _____.
c Nós [estar] _____.
d Eu [estar] _____.
e Elas [estar] _____.

▶ Dialogue 3

After their tennis game, Sylvia and Nelson chat over drinks.

Nelson Que outras cidades vai visitar?

Sylvia Bom, só me faltam seis semanas aqui, e quero visitar o sul.

Nelson Tem que visitar Rio Grande do Sul – a região dos gaúchos e as grandes fazendas. No sul também há bastante indústria.

Sylvia Sim, gostaria muito de ver Curitiba e também as cataratas de Iguaçu.

Nelson Vai adorar. Nesta época não tem tantos turistas – os meses piores são durante nosso verão – dezembro, janeiro e fevereiro.

Sylvia Ótimo. Então sem dúvida visitarei Iguaçu – são as mesmas cataratas que aparecem no filme 'A Missão' acerca dos jesuítas portugueses e suas atividades com os índios aqui.

Nelson Bom filme. Então, Sylvia, um brinde para o resto da sua viagem. Tchin tchin, e boa viagem.

Sylvia Saúde, e obrigada.

gaúchos (os)	cowboys/ranchers	janeiro	January
fazendas (as)	ranches/farms	fevereiro	February
indústria (a)	industry	sem dúvida	without doubt
cataratas (as)	waterfalls	as mesmas	the same
época (a)	season, time	A Missão	The Mission
tantos	so many	jesuítas (os)	Jesuits
turistas (os)	tourists	índios (os)	Indians
os meses piores	the worst months	brinde (o)	a toast
durante	during	o resto	the rest
verão (o)	summer	tchin tchin	cheers
dezembro	December	saúde	cheers

Grammar

outro, tanto, mesmo

All of these words change their endings depending on the nouns to which they are referring.

outro	outra	outros	outras	*other/s*
tanto	tanta	tantos	tantas	*so much/many*
mesmo	mesma	mesmos	mesmas	*same*

Tanto in this form only can also be used with verbs, to give more information about the action, e.g. **ela fala tanto** – *she talks so much*. This usage is known as the adverb. **Mesmo** can also mean *self*: **Ela mesma vai comprar a casa.** *She herself is going to buy the house.*

▶ Os meses The months

janeiro	January	julho	July
fevereiro	February	agosto	August
março	March	setembro	September
abril	April	outubro	October
maio	May	novembro	November
junho	June	dezembro	December

In Brazil they are generally written with a lower-case letter.

As estações do ano The seasons

o verão	summer	o outono	autumn
o inverno	winter	o primavera	spring

Remember that Brazil's summer coincides with winter in the northern hemisphere.

Celebratory expressions

tchin tchin/saúde	cheers
parabéns	congratulations
boa viagem	bon voyage
feliz aniversário	happy birthday
boa sorte	good luck
feliz Natal	Happy Christmas
feliz Ano Novo	Happy New Year
as melhoras	get well
boas férias	have a good holiday
feliz Páscoa	happy Easter

Summary

que vai fazer amanhã?	*what are you doing tomorrow?*
está livre amanhã/sábado?	*are you free tomorrow/ Saturday?*
gostaria de ver/visitar ...	*I'd like to see/visit ...*
leva uma hora/um mês	*it takes an hour/month*
estou livre a partir de ...	*I'm free from ...*
alô/quem fala?/daqui fala ...	*hello/who's speaking?/it's ... here*
a que horas nos encontramos?	*at what time shall we meet?*
estou viajando/trabalhando	*I'm travelling/working*
saúde/boa viagem	*cheers/bon voyage*
verão/outono/inverno/ primavera	*summer/autumn/winter/ spring*

Practice

5 Are these statements, based on Dialogue 3, **verdadeiro** or **falso**?

		T	F
a	Sylvia still has 7 weeks left in Brazil.		
b	Rio Grande do Sul is a region of farms and industry.		
c	At the moment there are not many tourists about.		
d	The worst months are in the spring.		
e	Sylvia wants to visit a Jesuit Mission.		
f	Nelson toasts the rest of Sylvia's journey.		

6 Look at the following situations and what people are saying. They have become mixed up. Can you decide which expression belongs with which picture?

i Feliz Páscoa   ii Feliz Aniversário   iii Feliz Natal
iv As Melhoras   v Parabéns   vi Boa Viagem

Do you understand?

Your friend has sent you a cutting from a paper about a place she would like to visit with you. Look at the piece and insert the correct words from the box to fill the gaps. Then answer the questions below.

flores festas Estados Unidos
novembro ano cores

1 What kind of activity is this (music/sport/nature)?
2 What can you see there?
3 What is new this year?
4 When was the event originally set up?

FLORES

Roselândia apresenta festas na primavera

da Redação

Acontecem até o próximo dia 17 de _____, na Roselândia (km 33 da rodovia Raposo Tavares), as _____ da Primavera e das Rosas.

Realizados desde 1954, os eventos mostram novidades em rosas, _____ e plantas ornamentais provenientes da Europa e dos _____ _____ que a Roselândia introduz no Brasil.

Neste _____, além dos jardins com novas variedades de rosas, a novidade são as petúnias, com 15 _____ diferentes.

Informações pelo tel. (011) 7924-0122. (SC)

15

como foi a viagem?

how was the journey?

In this unit you will learn
- how to talk in the past
- how to discuss a visit you have made
- how to describe actions

▶ Dialogue 1

Sylvia overhears some people talking about their holiday.

Sr Então, gostou da viagem? Visitou a catedral?

Sra Adorei. A catedral de lá é tão bonita e típica da arquitetura portuguesa. O nordeste é uma mistura interessante do africano com o europeu – a cultura, a música, e a religião.

Sr E as pessoas também – pele negra ao lado da branca, olhos pretos, azuis e verdes, cabelos escuros e claros – realmente é o que eles chamam uma miscelânia de culturas.

Sra Ficamos uma semana na Bahia, uns dias em Salvador e outros em Fortaleza. Assistimos a uma exibição de capoeira na praia, e falamos com os pescadores com suas jangadas.

Sr Comeram a comida de lá?

Sra Meu marido provou muitos pratos – vatapá por exemplo, mas eu achei um pouco picante.

Sr Então, valeu a pena?

Sra Sem dúvida! Esperamos voltar o ano que vem.

gostou?	did you enjoy?	**ficamos**	we stayed
visitou?	did you visit?	**assistimos a**	we watched
adorei	I loved	**capoeira (a)**	acrobatic dance
tão	so	**falamos**	we spoke
arquitetura (a)	architecture	**pescadores (os)**	fishermen
mistura (a)	mixture	**jangadas (as)**	Northeast boats
o africano	African	**comeram?**	did you (pl.) eat?
o europeu	European	**comida (a)**	food
cultura (a)	culture	**provou**	tasted
religião (a)	religion	**pratos (os)**	dishes
pessoas (as)	people	**achei**	I found/thought
pele negra	dark skin	**picante**	spicy
olhos (os)	eyes	**valeu a pena?**	was it worth it?
cabelos (os)	hair	**Esperamos**	we hope
sem dúvida	really, without doubt	**vatapá**	shrimp dish
o que eles chamam	what they call		

Exercise

Complete these statements with the correct ending:

1 The lady visited **a** the north. **b** the south. **c** the northeast.
2 In Bahia they stayed **a** a week. **b** a few days. **c** two days.
3 She thought the food was **a** too bitter. **b** too spicy. **c** too bland.

Grammar

The past

You have already met one or two expressions where the verb was in the past. To describe an action which was a one-off event, finished, complete, we use what is called the *simple past* (sometimes referred to as the preterite). In the dialogue, there were various examples, such as:

visitou *visited*   **ficamos** *we stayed*   **comeram** *you ate*

Let's look at how the simple past of the regular **-ar/-er/-ir** verbs is formed.

	remove infinitive ending	*add simple past endings*		*simple past*	
falar *to speak*	-ar	-ei	-amos	falei	falamos
		-ou	-aram	falou	falaram
comer *to eat*	-er	-i	-emos	comi	comemos
		-eu	-eram	comeu	comeram
partir *to depart/ leave/break*	-ir	-i	-imos	parti	partimos
		-iu	-iram	partiu	partiram

Can you spot ending patterns, like you did with the present tense? Notice e.g. **-amos/-emos/-imos**. Note that the Brazilian forms in the *we* person are the same in the present and the past tenses. You may have to deduce what time zone an event took place in by looking carefully at the context, and searching for clues, such as 'yesterday', 'last night', etc.

Ela falou comigo.   *She spoke with me.*
Comemos muito.   *We ate a lot.*
Partiram às nove horas.   *They (you pl.) left at nine o'clock.*

In Portuguese this tense also translates as *have, has done*. So **falei com ela** can be *I spoke to her*, or *I've spoken to her*.

Past questions

Did you notice the man's questions – **gostou?/visitou?/ comeram?** – simply used the past part of the verb, with no equivalent of the English *did*. So the questions actually say *you liked (enjoyed) …?/you visited …?/you ate …?*

O africano/o europeu

You have learnt that *o* + *adjective* is used to convey *the ... thing*, e.g. **o importante**. The examples in our dialogue here are very similar:

o africano – *that which is African*
o europeu – *that which is European*

This structure is much neater than the English phrase.

▶ Dialogue 2

Back in her hotel, Sylvia chats to the receptionist.

Recepcionista	Quando voltou de Porto Alegre?
Sylvia	Voltei ontem à noite. Apanhei o ônibus das 17 horas e cheguei aqui às 9:30.
Recepcionista	Gostou da visita?
Sylvia	Fiquei encantada. Visitamos uma fazenda, andamos a cavalo e comemos com os gaúchos.
Recepcionista	Comeu churrasco?
Sylvia	Sim, e bebemos um chimarrão, que é o chá típico da região.
Recepcionista	No inverno daqui, até os estudantes bebem este chá nas aulas por causa do frio daqui.
Sylvia	Que interessante. Bom. Tem algum recado para mim?
Recepcionista	Deixe ver. Ah sim, o senhor Ferreira acaba de telefonar. Disse que não é urgente.
Sylvia	Está bem, obrigada.

ontem à noite	*last night*	**recado (o)**	*message*
fiquei	*I became/was*	**acaba de**	*has just*
aulas (as)	*lessons*	**urgente**	*urgent*
por causa de	*because of*		

▶ Dialogue 3

Sylvia returns José's telephone call.

Sylvia	Alô, José?
José	Alô, Sylvia, tudo bem? Acabo de ligar para aí.
Sylvia	Eu sei. Me deram o recado agora.
José	Então, como foi a viagem pelo norte?

Sylvia	Foi ótima. Vi tantas coisas interessantes.
José	Foi a Manaus?
Sylvia	Fui, vi o teatro, dei uma voltinha pelo rio – fiz muitas coisas.
José	Foi à fazenda aí?
Sylvia	Sim, acabo de voltar. Os gaúchos são fascinantes – a maneira de viver, a cultura e o Fandango.
José	Dançou também?
Sylvia	Não me atrevi – eles dançam tão rapidamente, eu fiquei sentada.
José	Quando volta para cá?
Sylvia	Bom, amanhã vou para Curitiba, depois visitarei uma amiga num cafezal. Daqui a duas semanas estarei de volta em São Paulo.
José	Ligue para mim antes de partir.
Sylvia	Tchau.

acabo de ligar	*I've just rung*
deram	*they gave*
vi	*I saw*
fui	*I went*
dei uma voltinha	*I made a little trip*
maneira (a)	*way*
viver	*to live/living*
Fandango	*Fandango dance*
dançou?	*did you dance?*
não me atrevi	*I didn't dare*
dançam tão rapidamente	*they dance so quickly*
sentada	*sat down/seated*
cafezal (o)	*coffee plantation*
ligue para mim	*ring me*

Grammar

Past tense: awkward spellings

Some verbs alter their spellings in the past tense, to maintain certain sounds (hard or soft letters). In the dialogues you had: **cheguei** from **chegar**. Other similar examples are:

jogar – joguei   ficar – fiquei
pagar – paguei   explicar – expliquei
                    tocar – toquei *I played/touched*
                    indicar – indiquei

These changes happen in the first person singular only.

Other verbs also make changes in their spelling. Try to learn them as you come across them, and check in a grammar book for the patterns to learn.

Irregular simple past tense verbs

dar	dizer	fazer	estar	ir	poder	pôr
dei	disse	fiz	estive	fui	pude	pus
deu	disse	fez	esteve	foi	pôde	pôs
demos	dissemos	fizemos	estivemos	fomos	pudemos	pusemos
deram	disseram	fizeram	estiveram	foram	puderam	puseram

saber	sair	ser	ter	trazer	ver	vir
soube	saí	fui	tive	trouxe	vi	vim
soube	saiu	foi	teve	trouxe	viu	veio
soubemos	saímos	fomos	tivemos	trouxemos	vimos	viemos
souberam	saíram	foram	tiveram	trouxeram	viram	vieram

Acabar de To have just done

This handy expression is easy to learn, and very useful. You use the present tense of the verb **acabar** (*to finish*), plus **de** plus a verb in the infinitive. For example:

Sr Ferreira acaba de telefonar. *Mr Ferreira has just telephoned.*
Eu acabo de chegar. *I've just arrived.*

Aí There (where you are)

It is slightly confusing knowing when to use the various words for *here* and *there*.

aqui, cá *here*　　　**aí** *there*　　　**ali, lá** *there*
(where I am/we are)　(where you are)　(where neither of us are)

These also correspond to the demonstratives you learnt in Unit 13:

este *this here*　　**esse** *that near you*　　**aquele** *that over there*

So if you are talking to someone on the phone, you must use **aí** if you want to say e.g. *is it warm there?* – **está quente aí?** If you say **está quente lá?**, you are referring to somewhere distant from your listener.

Slow, slow, quick, quick, slow

Adverbs, as you learnt previously, give us more information about a verb. They answer the question *how?* For example:

They dance. How do they dance? Quickly.

In English many adverbs end in *-ly*.

Eles dançam. *Como* dançam? Rapidamente.

In Portuguese many adverbs end in -mente.

To form an adverb, take the feminine form of an adjective and add **-mente**. If there is no separate feminine form, add **-mente** to the standard form. For example:

rápido → rápida → rapida**mente**
fácil → facil**mente**

There are some irregular adverbs, including:

mal *badly*   **bem** *well*   **devagar** *slowly*   **cedo** *early*

Summary

gostou de ...?	*did you like (enjoy) ...?*
visitou a catedral/a praia?	*did you visit the cathedral/ beach?*
como foi a viagem?	*how was the trip?*
foi ótimo/maravilhoso/péssimo	*it was great/brilliant/awful*
voltei/apanhei/comi	*I returned/caught/ate*
tem algum recado para mim?	*do you have any messages for me?*
... acaba de telefonar/ligar	*... has just phoned*
daqui a duas semanas	*in two weeks' time*
falam rapidamente	*they speak quickly*
ligue para mim	*give me a ring/call*

Practice

1 Can you do the following?

   a Ask your friend if she visited the museum.
   b Say 'We stayed two weeks in Italy.'
   c Ask José and Sônia when they returned from New York.
   d Ask the receptionist if he has a message for you.
   e Say 'I've just arrived in the hotel.'
   f Say 'The Italians speak so quickly.'

2 Complete the sentences with the correct form of the past tense of the verb in brackets.

   a Ontem eu [comer] muito.
   b No ano passado eles [comprar] uma casa.
   c Nós [partir] à meia-noite.
   d Vocês [gostar] da festa?
   e Marcelo [escrever] um postal para sua mãe.

3 Choose the correct verb in each sentence.

   a Ela viu/veio João no mercado.
   b Eu fui/fiz um belo jantar.
   c Nós pudemos/pusemos os pratos na mesa.
   d Eles foram/fizeram ao cinema.
   e Você trouxe/teve boa sorte.

4 Complete your part of the dialogue about a visit.

Ricardo	Quando voltou do Rio?
You	(say *I returned yesterday afternoon. I arrived here at 3.25*)
Ricardo	Gostou da visita?
You	(say *yes, a lot. I walked on Copacabana beach, visited Sugar Loaf Mountain – Pão de Açúcar – and I saw the shanty towns – **as favelas**.*)
Ricardo	Gostou da comida também?
You	(say *yes, I ate **feijoada** and tried the firewater and lime drink.*)

5 Form the correct past tense and choose an adverb from the box to go with the pictures overleaf.

rapidamente	devagar	bem	cedo	mal

   a Eles [*lavantar-se*] _____.
   b Ela [*correr*] _____.
   c Elas [*cantar*] _____.
   d Nós [*falar*] _____.
   e Eu [*tocar piano*] _____.

6 ▶ Listen to the dialogue, and fill in the gaps with the words you hear.

José	Então, como foi a viagem para _____?
Sylvia	Foi ótima. Vi tantas coisas interessantes.
José	Foi a Londres?
Sylvia	Fui. Fui ao _____, vi o Big Ben, _____ o _____ – fiz muitas coisas.
José	Foi à _____ também?
Sylvia	Sim, acabo de voltar. Os _____ são _____ – a maneira de viver, a cultura e a _____.
José	Dançou também?
Sylvia	Não me atrevi – eles dançam tão rapidamente, eu fiquei sentada.
José	Quando volta para cá?
Sylvia	Bom, amanhã vou para _____, depois visitarei uma amiga. Daqui a _____ estarei de volta em _____.
José	Ligue para mim antes de partir. Tchau.
Sylvia	Tchau.

Do you understand?

Read Teresa's letter and see if you can answer the questions on it.

Minas, 10 de julho de 20 ..

Oi, Cecília, tudo bem?

Acabo de voltar das férias que passei nos Estados Unidos. Foi super-legal. Fiquei com meus tios, que moram na Califórnia. O tempo estava super-quente e gostei imensamente.

Fomos visitar muitos lugares interessantes, e vi as casas enormes dos atores de Hollywood. Passei em frente da casa de Michael Jackson - parece um castelo! Um dia viajamos até Disneyworld, onde passamos muitas horas divertindo-nos. Nunca vi tantas pessoas na vida! Provei a comida de lá - é tudo comida-rápida, tipo hamburguer e batatas, não é nada saudável. Comprei uma recordação para ti, acho que vai adorar.

Ouvi muita música americana, e na última noite fui a uma discoteca, que legal! A única coisa que realmente detestei foi a falta de guaraná!

Eu te digo mais no sábado, ligue para mim antes de vir,

tchau,

Teresa

1 Onde foi de férias?
2 Como estava o tempo?
3 Viu a casa de quem?
4 Que pensa da comida?
5 Onde foi na última noite?
6 Que detestou mais?
7 Quando vai ver Cecília?

16
quanto custaram?
how much did they cost?

In this unit you will learn
- how to talk about what you have bought
- how to identify your own property
- more about the past

▶ Dialogue 1

Sylvia listens to some people discussing what they have just bought.

Carlos Que quadros mais lindos! Onde os comprou?

Isabel Comprei-os numa lojinha no fim daquela rua ali. A senhora foi super-simpática comigo. Ela me deu um desconto porque comprei dois. Gosta, Paulo?

Paulo Gosto. São paisagens típicas do sul. Quanto custaram?

Isabel Não muito. Só 35 reais cada. Uma pechincha, não acham?

Carlos Realmente!

Isabel E você, Carlos, comprou alguma coisa?

Carlos Nós fomos até à feira hippy. Nunca vi tantas coisas bonitas. Que difícil escolher!

Isabel E daí – que decidiu?

Carlos Vi estas pedras preciosas, que adorei, e depois compramos esta caixinha de madeira.

Isabel Que bonitinha! Quanto custou? Foi cara?

Paulo Não, só 13 reais.

Isabel Puxa! Eu preciso ir lá já. Onde é que fica esta feira?

que quadros mais lindos!	*what beautiful pictures!*
lojinha (a)	*small shop*
no fim	*at the end*
simpática	*kind/nice*
paisagens (as)	*landscapes*
quanto custaram?	*how much did they cost?*
cada	*each (one)*
pechincha (a)	*a bargain*
a feira hippy	*hippy/craft fair*
nunca vi	*I've never seen*
escolher	*to choose*
e daí?	*and so?*
que decidiu?	*what did you decide?*
caixinha (a)	*small box*
foi cara?	*was it expensive?*
puxa!	*crikey!*

Exercise

Can you answer the following in Portuguese?

a Que comprou Isabel? _____

b Onde foram os dois senhores? _____

c O que Carlos adorou? _____

Grammar

Exclamations

It's nice to be able to inject exclamations into your dialogues, where relevant, as this makes your Portuguese much more authentic. Portuguese is a very expressive language, and the Brazilians especially love using it in a vibrant and sometimes vociferous way!

These few expressions will suffice for now to get you started:

Que + noun + adjective: **Que vestido lindo!** *What a nice dress!*
Or, using **mais**: **Que vestido mais lindo!** *What a gorgeous dress!*

Que coisa mais linda!	*What a lovely/gorgeous thing –* *isn't it gorgeous!* (very common)
Que legal!	*Cool/wicked!*
Ótimo!	*Great/cool/wicked*
Puxa!	*Gosh!*
Nossa!/Nossa Senhora	*Our Lady/crikey*
'Vij'/Virgem Maria	*Virgin Mary/flippin' heck* (quite strong)
E daí?	*And so/And then/And?/So what?*

Cada Each, every

Cada is a handy word meaning *each* or *every*. It never changes form, so you could have:

cada semana = **todas as semanas** *every week*
cada dia = **todos os dias** *every day*
cada um/uma custou *each one cost*

▶ Dialogue 2

A lady approaches the table.

Márcia Desculpem, mas acho que a senhora pegou meus óculos de sol. Deixei-os no balcão daquela loja de artesanato ali em cima há meia hora.

Regina O quê? Acho que a senhora está enganada. Estes óculos são meus.

Márcia Mas são óculos especiais porque não vejo muito bem. Olhe, aqui tem a marca Medioc.

Regina Onde? Ah, sim agora que eu vejo – tem razão. Peço desculpa. Foi sem querer. Então, onde estão os meus?

Ricardo	Aqui, na sua cesta. Que bagunceira!
Regina	Tem toda razão – Desculpe tá?
Márcia	Não importa. Bom dia.

desculpem	*excuse me (to more than one person)*	**são meus**	*they're mine*
		especiais	*special*
pegou	*you took*	**marca (a)**	*make*
balcão (o)	*counter*	**foi sem querer**	*I didn't mean to*
há meia hora	*half an hour ago*	**cesta (a)**	*basket*
enganada	*mistaken*	**que bagunceira!**	*what a mess-pot!*

Grammar

Há + time

You can use **há** + a time phrase to mean *ago*, e.g.

há meia hora	*half an hour ago*
há duas semanas	*two weeks ago*
há muito tempo	*a long time ago*

Identifying your belongings

In previous units you have practised the possessive adjectives *my, your, his, our,* etc. Remind yourself of them if you cannot remember them. To identify or claim your property, or that of someone else, you use the same set of words plus the verb **ser**:

| **estes óculos** *são* **meus** | *these glasses are mine* |
| **esta casa** *é* **nossa** | *this house is ours* |

You can answer the question **de quem é ...?** *Whose is ...?*, simply by saying:

é
são $\Big\}$ $\left\{\begin{array}{l} \text{meu/sua/nossos, etc.} \\ \text{de Maria} \\ \text{dele/dela, etc.} \end{array}\right.$

i Many towns in Brazil have a weekly crafts fair, often referred to as the **feira hippy**. Here you can find a variety of hand-made products, leather goods, jewellery, the beautiful semi-precious and precious stones for which Brazil is renowned, pictures – watercolour (**aquarela**) and oil (**óleo**) – and wax items (**de cera**). Also, there are usually stalls selling food: often you will find **baianas** – the typical women from Bahia (**o nordeste**), dressed in flouncy white clothes –

selling the kind of spicy food you would eat in Bahia. The **feira hippy** is a great place to buy presents, and a wonderful place to spend some time drifting around.

Summary

que ... mais lindo(s)!	*what beautiful ...!*
onde comprou?	*where did you buy (them/it)?*
quanto custou/custaram?	*how much did it/they cost?*
que difícil escolher!	*how difficult it is to choose!*
puxa!/que legal!	*crikey!/cool!*
acho que está enganado/a	*I think you're mistaken*
tem razão	*you're right*
foi sem querer	*it wasn't on purpose*
há uma hora/algum tempo	*an hour/some time ago*
é meu/minha, são meus/minhas	*it's/they're mine*

Practice

1 Replace **cada** with an appropriate form of **todo** (**o/a/os/as**), and change the verb forms where this becomes necessary.

   a Ela vai ao mercado [cada semana] _____.
   b Nós gostamos de viajar [cada ano] _____.
   c [cada um dos] _____ livros (custa) _____ R$10.
   d Maria trabalha muito [cada dia] _____.
   e [cada pessoa] _____ (ganha) _____ um presente.
   f Gosto de [cada mês] _____ do ano.

2 Fill in your part of this dialogue about an item you have bought.

Marco	Que vestido mais lindo. Onde o comprou?
You	(say *I bought it at the hippy-fair in the square.*)
Marco	Quanto custou?
You	(say *not a lot. Only 42 reais. Do you like it?*)
Marco	Gosto. Foi uma pechincha.
You	(Ask him *'did you buy anything?*)
Marco	Comprei este livro numa pequena livraria.
You	(say *what a most interesting book.*)

3 Complete the sentences with demonstratives (**este** etc.) and possessives according to the pictures and instructions.

a

Este _____ é _____. [*ours*]

b

_____ _____ são _____. [*mine*]

c

_____ _____ é _____ _____. [*of José*]

d

_____ _____ é _____. [*yours, of **você***]

e

_____ _____ são _____. [*theirs, of **eles***]

4 ▶ Listen to four people talking about when they did various activities, and fill in the table below.

Speaker	Did what?	How long ago?
1		
2		
3		
4		

Do you understand?

▶ Read the following dialogue and/or listen to it on the recording, then answer the questions on it.

Sra Desculpe, mas acho que o senhor pegou meu guarda-chuva. Deixei-o no restaurante Mineiro na praça há vinte minutos.

Sr O quê? Acho que a senhora está enganada. Este guarda-chuva é meu.

Sra Mas é um guarda-chuva especial. Olhe, aqui tem o nome da minha companhia – Empresa Tecnical Limitada.

Sr Onde? Ah, sim, agora que eu vejo – tem razão. Peço desculpa. Foi sem querer. Então, onde está o meu?

Sra Ali, ao lado da porta daquela loja.

Sr Você tem toda razão – Desculpe tá?

Sra Não importa. Bom dia.

1 What has he picked up by mistake?
2 Where was it left?
3 When?
4 How is it recognized?
5 Where is the other one?

era tudo tão diferente

it was all so different

In this unit you will learn
- how to talk about something you saw earlier
- how to identify a stranger
- how to recall how a place used to be

▶ Dialogue 1

Sylvia pops back to a shop to buy a skirt she had seen in the window, but finds the display has changed.

Empregada	Bom dia, pois não?
Sylvia	Havia uma saia na vitrine de que gostei muito, mas já não está mais lá.
Empregada	Como era a saia?
Sylvia	Era azul com flores pequenas.
Empregada	E onde estava exatamente?
Sylvia	Estava à esquerda da vitrine, bem na frente.
Empregada	E era de algodão ou de lã?
Sylvia	De algodão. Era muito bonita. Acho que custava 56 reais.
Empregada	Ah, sim, agora estou me lembrando. Só tinha aquela e mais duas daquele modelo, e vendemos as três hoje de manhã.
Sylvia	Ai, que pena!
Empregada	Quer ver as outras saias que temos?
Sylvia	Não, obrigada. Só queria aquela.
Empregada	Está bem. Talvez haja mais na semana que vem.
Sylvia	Está bem.

havia	*there was*	**estou me**	
vitrine (a)	*shop window*	**lembrando**	*I'm remembering*
já não está			
mais lá	*it's no longer there*	**tinha**	*there was*
era	*it was*	**modelo (o)**	*style*
flores (as)	*flowers*	**vendemos**	*we sold*
estava	*it was*	**que pena!**	*what a pity*
bem na frente	*right in front*	**queria**	*I wanted*
custava	*it cost*	**talvez haja**	*perhaps there will be*

Grammar

Há ... havia There is/are ... there was/were ...

Havia is the past equivalent of **há**. Remember you can use **há** to mean *there is/are*. Therefore, **havia** can mean *there was/were*. You may also come across the word **houve**, also meaning *there was/were*, but used to describe one-off happenings, such as:

houve um acidente	*there was an accident*
houve um barulho enorme	*there was a huge noise*
havia muitas pessoas na rua	*there were many people in the street*

Brazilians also use parts of **ter** for the same purpose, e.g. **teve um acidente/tinha muitas pessoas.**

The past, part 2

In Unit 15 you learnt how to use the simple past to describe actions in the past which had been completed. In the dialogue here you are introduced to another past tense, called the *imperfect*. Try to remember it as *imperfect* because usually there is no perfect ending to it – it's more open-ended than the previous past tense. It describes an action which was continuous in the past, going on for some time. Look at the examples from the dialogue:

Como era? (from **ser**)	*What was it like?* (all the time)
Onde estava? (**estar**)	*Where was it?* (all the time it was in the window)
Custava	*It cost* (all the time it had a price)
Só queria esta	*I only wanted this one* (all the time)

Compare these with verbs in the simple past:

| **Como foi o filme?** | *What was the film like?* (as a whole) |
| **Ele me custou** | *It cost me* (one-off payment) |

It may help to look at the following 'time-line'.

imperfect   simple past   NOW

The imperfect is a continuous line in the past, with often no clear ending (this can continue right up to the present time – *I wanted it and I still do*). The simple past is safely enclosed in a solid, complete box – it's finished. Often the simple past will interrupt an imperfect one, such as:

I was having a bath WHEN   *the phone rang.*
(continuous)   (sudden point)   (simple past)

bathing   phone

Formation

	remove infinitive ending	add imperfect endings		imperfect	
falar *to speak*	-ar	-ava	-ávamos	falava	falávamos
		-ava	-avam	falava	falavam
comer *to eat*	-er	-ia	-íamos	comia	comíamos
		-ia	-iam	comia	comiam
partir *to depart/ leave/break*	-ir	-ia	-íamos	partia	partiámos
		-ia	-iam	partia	partiam

e.g. **Ela falava comigo.** *She was speaking to me.*

Watch out for these irregular verbs:

pôr *to put*   punha, punha, púnhamos, punham
ser *to be*   era, era, éramos, eram
ter *to have*   tinha, tinha, tínhamos, tinham
vir *to come*   vinha, vinha, vínhamos, vinham

▶ Dialogue 2

Sylvia has had a visitor at her hotel.

Recepcionista Senhora Peters, havia um senhor aqui que a procurava.
Sylvia Um senhor? Como era?
Recepcionista Era bastante alto, tinha cabelo preto, e um bigode, e estava vestido de terno cinzento.
Sylvia Como ele se chamava?
Recepcionista Não sei. Não disse o nome.
Sylvia Mas o que ele queria?
Recepcionista Também não sei. Só disse que voltava mais tarde.
Sylvia Ele tinha que idade?
Recepcionista Bom, provavelmente 50 e tantos anos.
Sylvia Ah, já sei quem era. É o pai duma amiga minha que tem um cafezal aqui. Vou ficar uns dias com a família dela. Bom, vou subir.

procurava	*was looking for*
como era?	*what was he like?*
bastante	*quite*
alto	*tall*
bigode (o)	*moustache*
vestido	*dressed*
terno (o)	*suit*
como ele se chamava?	*What was he called?*
voltava	*he would return*
idade (a)	*age*
provavelmente	*probably*
50 e tantos anos	*50-odd*
pai (o)	*father*
uma amiga minha	*a friend of mine*
subir	*to go up (stairs)*

Grammar

People descriptions

Notice which verbs were used in the descriptions.

era from **ser** – for permanent characteristics
tinha from **ter** – possession, hair/eyes/beards, etc., age
estava from **estar** – temporary characteristics/states, what they
are wearing

If you want to describe people in detail, you will need:

height	**alto** *tall*	**médio** *medium*	**baixo** *small, short*	
build	**grande** *large*	**gordo** *fat*	**forte** *strong*	**pequeno** *small*
	magro *thin*			
eyes	**os olhos** + colour			
hair	**o cabelo** + colour	**comprido** *long*	**curto** *short*	
	liso *straight*			
extras	**bigode** *moustache*	**barba** *beard*	**óculos** *glasses*	
	careca *bald*			
clothes	revise Unit 7			

Uma amiga minha A friend of mine

To express *a ... of mine/of yours*, etc. place the noun first,
followed by the appropriate possessive. For example:

uns sapatos seus	*some shoes of yours/his, etc.*
uma amiga nossa	*a friend of ours*

▶ Dialogue 3

Sr Mendes shows Sylvia round the coffee plantation, and explains how things used to be.

Sr Mendes	Tudo é muito diferente agora. Antigamente havia menos tecnologia, não havia tantas máquinas, e mais pessoas trabalhavam por aqui.
Sylvia	Mas, não é mais fácil hoje em dia?
Sr Mendes	Isso, sim, mas também é um pouco mais impessoal. Antes a gente falava muito, comíamos juntos, íamos a bailes nas outras fazendas, e ajudávamos uns aos outros. Hoje existe muito mais competição.
Sylvia	E a cidade, mudou também?
Sr Mendes	Mudou, sim. Todos os dias íamos ao centro, tomar um cafezinho, falar com os amigos, e depois jogávamos cartas e a vida passava na valsa. Hoje é tudo movimento, rápido, dinheiro.
Sylvia	Mas pelo menos tem uma bela fazenda.
Sr Mendes	Sim, casa, família, boa comida e um estilo de vida que não tínhamos antes – sim, tudo tem recompensa. Vamos ver os processos lá dentro?
Sylvia	Vamos, e depois um bom cafezinho!

antigamente	*before*	**jogávamos**	*we used to play*
tecnologia (a)	*technology*	**movimento (o)**	*rush*
máquinas (as)	*machines*	**dinheiro (o)**	*money*
trabalhavam	*they used to work*	**pelo menos**	*at least*
impessoal	*impersonal*	**bela**	*lovely*
íamos	*we used to go*	**tínhamos**	*we had*
bailes (os)	*dances*	**recompensa (a)**	*reward*
existe	*there exists*	**processos (os)**	*processes*
competição (a)	*competition*	**mudou**	*it has changed*
a vida passava na valsa	*life went with the flow*		
ajudávamos uns aos outros	*we used to help one another*		
um estilo de vida	*lifestyle*		

Grammar

The imperfect – the way we used to be

Another function of the imperfect tense is to describe how things 'used to be' or things you 'used to do'. You can introduce statements with expressions like:

antes/antigamente/ no passado	*before/in the past*
quando era/éramos jovem/ jovens	*when I/you/he was/we were young*
quando morávamos em ...	*when we used to live in ...*

Look at these examples:

Quando João morava na Índia, bebia chá todos os dias.	*When John lived (used to live) in India, he drank (used to drink) tea every day.*
Antes de me casar, eu trabalhava num banco.	*Before I married, I worked (used to work) in a bank.*

Summary

havia ...	*there was/were ...*
já não mais está (lá)	*it's no longer (there)*
como era?	*what was it like?*
onde estava?	*where was it?*
só queria este/esta	*I only wanted this one*
o que (ele) queria?	*what did (he) want?*
era alto/gordo/forte	*he was tall/fat/strong (large)*
50 e tantos anos	*50-odd/50-ish*
antigamente dançávamos	*we used to dance in the past*
um amigo meu/seu/nosso	*a friend of mine/yours/ours*

Practice

1 Now can you do the following?

   a Say *there was a blouse I liked in the shop window.*
   b Say *it was on the right of the display.*
   c Say *she was short, with long hair and blue eyes.*
   d Say *he was probably 40 or so years old.*
   e Ask *is it not more interesting nowadays?*
   f Say *we used to swim every day.*

2 Decide in each case whether the verb should be in the imperfect or the preterite (simple past) tense.

   a Ontem eu **fui/ia** à cidade para comprar um selo.
   b Quando **era/foi** jovem, Carlos fumava.
   c Nós **jantamos/jantávamos** quando o telefone tocou.
   d Antigamente eles **comiam/comeram** muito mal.
   e Na semana passada ela **veio/vinha** à minha casa.
   f Onde **estava/esteve** você quando eu te telefonei?

3 Listen to descriptions of people, and decide which articles of clothing go on each body.

4 Form the correct part of the imperfect tense for the verbs, and link them to the second part of the sentence.

Quando éramos jovens ...

a ir _____   i   mais energia.
b brincar _____   ii aos bailes.
c ter _____   iii férias com nossos pais.
d estudar _____   iv no campo.
e passar _____   v   todos os dias.

5 Complete your part in this dialogue in a shop.

You (Say *there was a shirt in the shop window, but it's not there now.*)

Emp. Como era?

You (Say *it was black and was made of wool.*)

Emp. E onde estava exatamente?

You (Say *it was on the left of the display, behind the trousers.*)

Emp.	Ah sim, lamento, mas vendemos aquela ontem. Quer ver os outros modelos que temos?
You	(Say *no thanks. I only wanted that one*.)
Emp.	Está bem. Adeus.

6 Link up the following descriptions with the correct pictures.

i ii iii iv

a João é alto e forte. Tem cabelo curto e liso e um bigode. Está vestido de terno e chapéu.

b Sabrina é de estatura média e magra. Tem cabelo comprido. Usa óculos.

c Lúcia é baixa e um pouco gorda. O cabelo dela é liso e curto, e ela está vestida de saia e blusa.

d Maurício é alto e magro. É careca.

Do you understand?

Read this excerpt from an interview with a Brazilian Indian, and decide which verbs from the two boxes should fill each gap: you must choose between verbs in the imperfect and preterite (simple past) tenses. Then answer the questions which follow.

| era | defendia | brigava | estavam |

| cheguei | criei | achei |
| consegui | veio | começamos |

O ÍNDIO JURUNA COM A PALAVRA

(Trechos de uma entrevista publicada no 'Folhetim', suplemento do jornal 'Folha de São Paulo', de 25-12-1977, gravada pelos jornalistas Sérgio Gomes, João Marcos Pereira e Cristina Vilares)

'Estou com três anos como chefe. Antes eu 1 ____ chefe de batalhador, o chefe guerreiro, 2 ____ todo o povo índio, porque naquele tempo a gente 3 ____ muito. Quando eu 4 ____ aí eu tirei todas as brigas. Depois eu 5 ____ outro problema: da reserva. Eu estava sabendo que 800 índios 6 ____ vivendo com 14 mil hectares. Então eu 7 ____ muito pouco. Eu conheço também os limites, conheço mapa, mais ou menos, então eu achei muito pequena essa reserva. Aí eu aumentei para 180 mil hectares. Vou lutando e defendendo o direito do povo do Xavante. Eu falava com o governador do Mato Grosso, eu falava com o presidente do Incra, com o presidente da Funai, eu brigava com o Ministério do Interior. Falava com o vice-presidente da República. 8 ____ o presidente, parece Costa e Silva, criou o decreto da terra dos Xavantes. Depois 9 ____ o dr. Emílio também decretou outra vez. O presidente Geisel fez sair todo o mundo: tirou fazendeiro, tirou posseiro, tirou tudo. Nós 10 ____ marcar limite, assim com picada, para poder tirar o pessoal.'

| | | T | F |

a He has been the chief for three years.
b When he arrived, 800 indians were living on 14,000 hectares of land.
c He thought the reserve was too big.
d He spoke to the President of Brazil.
e The land was designated Xavante land.
f The text is taken from a TV interview.

18

o que você tem?

what's the matter?

In this unit you will learn
- how to describe illness and ailments
- how to deal with the chemist and doctor
- how to cope with an accident
- how to say goodbye

▶ Dialogue 1

Sylvia has returned to the Ferreira's house in São Paulo, but has woken up not feeling very well.

Sylvia Marli, não me sinto nada bem.
Marli O que você tem?
Sylvia Estou com dor de barriga e tenho uma dor de cabeça.
Marli Parece muito pálida. Vou chamar nosso médico. Fique aí na cama até ele chegar.

[40 minutos mais tarde]

Médico Onde dói, senhora Peters?
Sylvia A barriga e a cabeça. Os olhos também me doem.
Médico Que comeu ontem?
Sylvia Ontem à noite saímos para um restaurante e eu comi um arroz com mariscos.
Médico E em geral tem algum problema quando come peixe?
Sylvia Geralmente não. É grave?
Médico Não se preocupe, senhora Peters. Creio que é só uma pequena alergia. Fique onde está, na cama, até sábado, e tome este medicamento.

não me sinto nada bem	*I don't feel at all well*
o que você tem?	*what's the matter?*
me dói/doem ...	*my ... hurts/hurt*
barriga (a)	*belly*
dor (a)	*pain*
cabeça (a)	*head*
pálida	*pale*
médico (o)	*doctor*
fique	*stay*
cama (a)	*bed*
até ele chegar	*until he arrives*
saímos	*we went out*
um arroz com mariscos	*seafood risotto*
grave	*serious*
não se preocupe	*don't worry*
creio que	*I think/believe that*
alergia (a)	*allergy/reaction*
medicamento (o)	*medication*

True or false?

Mark these statements **verdadeiro** or **falso**.

		V	F
a	Sylvia has a sore stomach.		
b	Her teeth also hurt.		
c	Last night she ate steak and rice.		

Grammar

1 Feeling ill

To express ailments, you can use the verb **doer** *to hurt* in the following way:

indirect object pronoun + **doer** + part/s of body

me	**dói**	**a cabeça** = *my head hurts*
lhe	**docm**	**os olhos** = *his/her/your eyes hurt*

What you are doing is saying that x gives pain to you/him, etc.

You can also use: **ter uma dor de ...**
ter uma dor em (no, na, nos, nas) ...
estar com dor de/no, na, nos, nas ...

These are most common in Brazil.

Tenho uma dor de cabeça.	*I have a headache.*
Ele tem uma dor nos olhos.	*He has sore eyes.*

Other ailments may include:

uma enxaqueca	*a migraine*
ter gripe	*to have a cold*
ter insolação	*to have sunstroke*
cortar	*to cut*
magoar	*to hurt*
bater	*to hit*

O corpo The body

You cannot describe where your pain is adequately without knowing the parts of the body. On the next page is a body and head for you to study.

▶ Dialogue 2

When she goes to the chemist (**a farmácia**) to pick up Sylvia's medicine, Marli overhears another customer.

Farmacêutico	Bom dia. Diga por favor.
Cliente	Tem alguma coisa para dor de garganta?
Farmacêutico	Sim, temos estas pastilhas que são excelentes, ou este xarope.
Cliente	Levo as pastilhas.
Farmacêutico	É só?
Cliente	Não, o que tem para queimaduras de sol?
Farmacêutico	Hmm, este creme é bom. É só 2 reais e 40 centavos.
Cliente	Bom, levo dois frascos.
Farmacêutico	Então, são 7 reais e 80 centavos.
Cliente	Também preciso de alguma coisa para meus lábios – estão muito secos.
Farmacêutico	Tem isto, que é novo – é um batom transparente

que protege o lábio antes e depois do sol.
Cliente Muito bem. Vou experimentar.
Farmacêutico Agora são 8 reais e 45 centavos. Adeus e espero que melhore!

tem alguma coisa para ...?	*do you have anything for ...?*
garganta (a)	*throat*
pastilhas (as)	*pastilles*
xarope (o)	*syrup*
o que tem para ...?	*what do you have for ...?*
queimaduras de sol	*sunburn*
creme (o)	*cream*
lábios (os)	*lips*
secos	*dry*
novo	*new*
batom (o)	*lipstick*
protege	*protects*
antes e depois do sol	*before and after sun*

Grammar

Medicines

Here are a few useful items you may need to purchase at the chemist's:

comprimidos	*pills*
uma ligadura	*bandage*
toalhas higiênicas	*sanitary towels*
repelente de insetos	*insectant repellant*
aspirina	*aspirin*
um band-aid	*plaster*
um colírio	*eyewash*
antihistamínico	*antihistamine*

Subjunctive verbs

The expression **Espero que melhore** *I hope that you get well* (*better*) introduces us to another area of verbs in Portuguese, which is extremely complex, and which causes the most concern to learners as they progress a little further. We are only going to touch lightly upon it as an introduction.

So far, you have learnt some different tenses of verbs, to help you talk in various time zones. Now we are going to look at something called the *subjunctive*, which also has a set of tenses, but used in very different, and specific, circumstances. One of these, in the present tense, is used, as you saw in the dialogue, after the verb *to hope*, or *to wish*, when you are wishing something for someone else.

It is also used after:

esperar *que*	*to hope/wish that*
duvidar *que*	*to doubt that*
sentir *que*	*to feel sorry that*
é possível *que*	*it is possible that*
é incrível *que*	*it is incredible that*
é provável *que*	*it is probable that*

The main feature is the word **que**, and it is the verb which *follows* **que** that goes into the subjunctive form. You have in fact come across the subjunctive before, in the guise of commands. Remember in Unit 7, you learnt how the endings of -**ar** verbs became like -**er** verbs, and those of -**er** and -**ir** verbs became like -**ar** ones? That is the formation of the present subjunctive. Here again to remind you are our three regular verbs:

	subjunctive			
falar *to speak*	fale	fale	falemos	falem
comer *to eat*	coma	coma	comamos	comam
partir *to depart/leave/break*	parta	parta	partamos	partam

As usual, watch out for irregulars! Look at these examples:

Espero que você coma bem.	*I hope that you eat well.*
Ela duvida que ele parta amanhã.	*She doubts that he will depart tomorrow.*
É impossível que elas escrevam tanto.	*It's impossible that they (should) write so much.*

The subjunctive is something that takes a long time to sink in, but at least with a small notion of it under your belt, you are armed to understand a little bit more about the structures that may be used in conversation with you.

▶ Dialogue 3

On the way back home Marli witnesses an accident. She goes over to the injured person.

Marli Você precisa de ajuda?
Sr Obrigado. Tenho uma dor na perna. Acho que está partida. Que dor! Não posso mexer nada.
Marli Que aconteceu?
Sr Eu estava atravessando a rua sem problemas; tinha chegado mais ou menos ao centro quando de repente – baf! – um carro me bateu e aqui estou.
Marli Parece que o carro não parou. Idiota! Bom, não se preocupe, senhor. Vou chamar uma ambulância. Não demora muito.

Marli uses the telephone in a nearby shop.

Marli Alô, escute, houve um acidente na rua Moraes Sales.
Telefonista Tem alguém ferido?
Marli Sim, um senhor, a perna foi quebrada quando um carro a bateu. Precisamos duma ambulância.
Telefonista Onde está exatamente?
Marli Na rua Moraes Sales perto da praça Paulista, ao lado da igreja Santa Augusta. O nome do senhor é Paulo Mendonça.
Telefonista E seu nome senhora?
Marli Eu sou Marli Ferreira.
Telefonista Está bem. Uma ambulância está a caminho.

ajuda (a)	help
mexer	to move
que aconteceu?	what happened?
estava atravessando	was crossing
tinha chegado	had arrived
de repente	suddenly
bateu	hit
quebrada, partida	broken
parou	stopped
idiota (o)	idiot
demora	take a while
escute	listen
ferido	injured
foi quebrada	was broken
está a caminho	is on the way

Grammar

Imperfect

In Unit 14 you saw how you could use the verb **estar** plus the gerund – the 'ing' part of the verb (**-ando/-endo/-indo**) – to make an action that is currently happening. You can also do this using the imperfect of **estar** and the gerund to describe an action in the past which was in the middle of happening, e.g. **Estava atravessando** *I was crossing*. This is used more commonly than the pure imperfect on its own – **atravessava** *I was crossing*.

The past, part 3

If you want to describe an action which took place and was completed before another past action began, you use a tense known as the *pluperfect*. In English it corresponds to *had done*. Look at these examples in English:

> *When he arrived home, she had (already) gone out.*

> *We were sure he had told us a lie.*

And from the dialogue:

> **Tinha chegado ... quando de repente ...**   *I had arrived ... when suddenly ....*

This tense is often used in relating incidents, or giving a report of a sequence of events.

It is formed using the imperfect of **ter**, plus the past participle. For example:

> **Eles tinham comido muito.**   *They had eaten a lot.*
> **Maria tinha falado com ele antes de sair.**   *Maria had spoken with him before going out.*

The passive

With most actions, there are two ways of expressing what has happened. Look at these two examples:

1   **Paulo quebrou a perna.**   *Paul broke his leg.*
2   **A perna foi quebrada (por ...)**   *The leg was broken (by ...).*

Statement **1** is known as an *active sentence*, where the subject of the verb actively carries out the action. Statement **2** is called a *passive sentence*, because the object in fact becomes the subject, or is acted upon by someone or something, known as the agent.

The passive is constructed using **ser** plus the past participle of the relevant verb, used as an adjective. If you want to say who or what the agent was/is, you introduce it with **por** *by*. For example:

A janela foi fechada pela professora. — *The window was closed by the teacher.*
Os soldados foram mortos. — *The soldiers were killed.*
Eu fui mordido por uma abelha. — *I was stung by a bee.*

estar and the past participle used as an adjective conveys the *state* something is in as a result of an action, e.g.

A janela estava fechada. — *The window was closed.*
Ele estava perdido. — *He was lost.*

Practice

1 Can you now:

   a Say that you don't feel at all well.
   b Ask your husband/wife where it hurts.
   c Ask if the chemist has anything for toothache.
   d Ask what he has for migraines.
   e Ask what has happened.
   f Tell the emergency services that there's been an accident on Campo street.

2 Link up the statements on the next page with the pictures below.

a Tem alguma coisa para insolação?
b Dói-me a barriga.
c João bateu o dedo.
d Ele tem uma dor nos olhos.
e Meu marido tem uma dor de cabeça.
f Cortei a perna. Preciso dum band-aid.

3 Link up the two parts of each sentence, and form the second verb (in brackets) in the subjunctive.

a Esperamos que
b Sinto muito que
c É incrível que
d Ela duvida que
e É possível que
f Espero que

i eles [estudar] tanto.
ii nós [ganhar] muito dinheiro.
iii sua filha [melhorar].
iv Sonia [estar] doente.
v ele me [amar].
vi ele [vir] hoje.

4 ▶ Listen to the phone call to the emergency services and write down the following information.

| Accident where? | How many | Injuries? | Exact |
| Name of caller? | injured? | | location? |

5 Place the correct past form of the verb and give any other information required to complete the sentences.

a A escola **ser/estar** _____ [closed] _____ durante as férias.
b Os presentes **ser/estar** _____ [given] _____ aos turistas [by the hotel owner] _____ _____.
c As portas **ser/estar** _____ [open] _____.
d Eu **ser/estar** _____ [invited] _____.
e A carta **ser/estar** _____ [written] _____ [by Luis] _____ _____.
f Os sapatos **ser/estar** _____ muito [dirty] _____.

6 Complete your part of the dialogue at the chemist's.

You (Ask the pharmacist do you have anything for a headache?)
Farm. Sim, temos estas aspirinas que são boas, ou tem estes comprimidos.
You (Say I'll take the aspirins.)
Farm. É só?
You (Say no, what do you have for allergies?)
Farm. Tem este creme repelente, se é alergia a insetos, ou estes comprimidos antihistamínicos.

You	(Say *I'll take a bottle of the cream. How much is that please?*)
Farm.	São 6 reais e 40 centavo, por favor.
You	(Say *thank you and goodbye.*)

i It's advisable to have any injections before you get to Brazil, drink only bottled water and avoid any shellfish, which may not be freshly caught. Chemists can be extremely helpful; hospital treatment is chaotic, although there is an excellent hospital in São Paulo. Most medication is available, but take supplies if you are travelling inland or into the Amazon.

Avoid undue contact with police if you can help it!

▶ Dialogue 4

It's time for Sylvia to leave. The Ferreiras have taken her to the airport and are saying goodbye.

José	Sylvia, foi tão bom te ver outra vez. Volte logo – sabe que tem uma casa aqui sempre. Será sempre bem-vinda.
Sylvia	Obrigada, José. E Marli também, obrigada por tudo. Foi uma visita fantástica, e vocês foram muito generosos. Espero-os lá na Inglaterra, tá? A próxima vez vocês vão ficar conosco.
Marli	Foi um prazer te conhecer finalmente. José tinha falado tanto em ti. Volte sempre, e nossos cumprimentos ao resto da família. Leve consigo estes CDs da nossa música.
Sylvia	Que legal! Gilberto Gil, Milton Nascimento, Simone, alguns dos meus músicos preferidos. Obrigada e até à próxima.
José	Se Deus quiser.
Sylvia	E se eu ganhar na loteria! Adeus. Tchau, tchau!

volte logo	come back soon
por tudo	for everything
generosos	kind
foi um prazer	it was a pleasure
finalmente	finally
em ti	about you
músicos preferidos (os)	favourite singers
se Deus quiser	hopefully/God willing
se eu ganhar na loteria	If I win the lottery
volte sempre	come back again

Summary

não me sinto nada bem	*I don't feel at all well*
o que você tem?	*what's the matter?*
me dói/doem	*my ... hurt/s*
não se preocupe	*don't worry*
tem alguma coisa para ...?	*do you have anything for ...?*
o que tem para ...?	*what do you have for ...?*
espero que melhore	*I hope you get better*
que aconteceu?	*what (has) happened?*
houve um acidente	*there's been an accident*
volte sempre	*come back (again)*

Congratulations on completing
Teach Yourself Brazilian Portuguese!

I hope you have enjoyed working your way through the course. I am always keen to receive feedback from people who have used my course, so why not contact me and let me know your reactions? I'll be particularly pleased to receive your praise, but I should also like to know if you think things could be improved. I always welcome comments and suggestions and I do my best to incorporate constructive suggestions into later editions.

You can contact me through the publishers at: Teach Yourself Books, Hodder Headline Ltd, 338 Euston Road, London NW1 3BH, or c/o The Adult College, White Cross Education Centre, Quarry Road, Lancaster LA1 3SE.

I hope you will want to build on your knowledge of Portuguese and have made a few suggestions to help you do this in the section entitled **Taking it further** on page 202.

Boa sorte, e força!

Sue Tyson-Ward

In this unit you will have further practice on the grammatical points and vocabulary items from Units 1–9. You may wish to revise the Grammar sections before you begin, or use this unit as a progress test. All the answers are in the Key on p. 213.

1 Decide which article is required for each noun, and tick the appropriate boxes.

	o	a	os	as
livro				
casa				
filhas				
prato				
jornais				
	um	**uma**	**uns**	**umas**
cidade				
senhores				
ruas				
país				
estação				

2 Supply the correct form of the demonstrative (**este** or **aquele**) in each case.

a _____ livro que tenho é francês.
b _____ hotéis ali na praça são muito bons.
c Gosta d_____ casas aqui?
d _____ senhora é minha amiga.

3 Use the correct form of **todo** (**tudo**) etc.

a _____ é muito interessante aqui.
b _____ minhas amigas estudam português.
c Ela não gosta de _____ o filme.

d Quero comprar _____ a roupa.

e Nós adoramos _____ neste país.

f _____ as semanas vou ao cinema.

4 Write out the Portuguese for these numbers.

a	36	f	12,654
b	152	g	25,999
c	500	h	100,000
d	1,321	i	14
e	5,800	j	95

5 What are these numbers?

a oitocentos e noventa e nove

b setecentos e vinte e três

c quatrocentos e sessenta e oito

d dois mil, quinhentos e um

e quatro mil, oitocentos e dois

f sete mil, quinhentos e cinqüenta e quatro

g onze mil e cem

h sessenta e oito mil, trezentos e trinta e seis

i cento e cinco

j trezentos e sete

6 Form the present tense correctly.

a Eles não [comer] _____ carne.

b Eu [falar] _____ alemão.

c Você [ir] _____ ao trabalho?

d Ela não [partir] _____ hoje.

e Nós [fazer] _____ muito barulho.

f João [viajar] _____ todos os meses.

g Vocês não [escrever] _____ muitas cartas.

h Os senhores [compreender] _____?

7 Decide in each case whether the verb should be **ser**, **estar** or **ficar**, and write the correct form.

a Ela [   ] francesa.

b Onde [   ] minha bolsa?

c O banco [   ] ao lado do museu.

d As chaves [   ] em cima da mesa.

e Todas as lojas [   ] muito perto do centro.

f Eles [   ] engenheiros.

g O apartamento [   ] no segundo andar.

h João [   ] meu amigo.

8 Make up whole sentences by selecting an appropriate form of **ter** or **haver** and using a suitable ending.

a	Meu irmão	temos	i	um bom carro.
b	Na cidade	têm	ii	quinze anos.
c	Nós	tem	iii	para beber?
d	O que	há	iv	meu livro?
e	Não	tem	v	muitas pessoas.
f	Júlia e Maria	há	vi	fome.
g	Você	tenho	vii	lojas interessantes.
h	Na praça	há	viii	uma casa grande.

In the Key you will find suggested sample answers.

9 Form the correct part of the command in each phrase.

a Falar [sing.] mais devagar.
b Comer [sing.] menos.
c Fechar [sing.] a porta.
d Não abrir [plur.] as janelas.
e Beber [plur.] mais água.
f Não subir [plur.] estas escadas.
g Começar [sing.] agora.
h Preencher [sing.] esta ficha.

10 Follow the clues to fill in the crossword on nationalities and countries.

Across: 1 Pessoas dos Estados Unidos.
        2 O país dos ingleses.
        3 A língua dos espanhois.
        4 Rio é no ...
Down: 5 Paris é o capital da ...
        6 Vêm da Alemanha.
        7 Da Grécia.
        8 País dos italianos.
        9 Pessoa da China.
      10 Os alemães vêm da ...

11 Can you complete these words, which are all items of clothing?

a v------
b s---
c c--ç--

d --p-t-
e --m--a
f b-u--

g -h---u
h l-v--
i c-s---
j g----t-

12 Can you find nine colours in this wordsearch?

V	E	R	M	E	L	H	O
E	O	O	T	P	A	M	C
R	L	X	B	C	O	D	N
D	E	O	P	R	E	F	A
E	R	F	R	G	O	H	R
A	A	A	E	B	C	S	B
A	M	Z	T	L	U	Z	A
Q	A	N	O	J	P	T	W

13 Follow the clues and complete the crossword on shops and facilities.

Across: 1 Grande loja.
2 Para trocar dinheiro ...
6 Onde se compram botas, sapatos, etc.
7 Onde se vendem frutas, legumes, peixe ...
8 Fica na rua – para comprar jornais, mapas, revistas.

Down: 3 Para comprar selos ...
4 Onde se compra carne.
5 Onde se compram livros.
9 Para comer e beber ...
10 Onde se vê um filme.

In this unit you will have further practice on the grammatical points and vocabulary items from Units 10–18. You may wish to revise the Grammar sections before you begin, or use this unit as a progress test. All the answers are in the Key on pp. 213–14.

1 Form adverbs from the words in brackets.

    a   [súbito] _____ vi meu amigo na praça.
    b   [final] _____ os alunos terminaram o exame.
    c   Sai daqui [imediato] _____!
    d   Não entendo esta língua [fácil] _____.
    e   [aparente] _____, ela só tem treze anos!
    f   Ela está [temporário] _____ fora do país.
    g   Os dois irmãos cantam muito [mau] _____.

2 Change the verbs from the present tense to the preterite.

    a   Elas não [compreendem] _____ muito.
    b   Todos os trenes [partem] _____ tarde.
    c   Eu [vendo] _____ fotografias.
    d   Maria e Sonia [chegam] _____ de táxi.
    e   Pedro [está] _____ no hospital.
    f   Vocês [percebem] _____ tudo?
    g   Você [tem] _____ dinheiro?
    h   [tiramos] _____ as malas do hotel.

3 Form the imperfect tense correctly in these examples.

    a   Quantos anos [ter] _____ você quando foi para a Alemanha?
    b   Durante as férias nós [acordar] _____ tarde todos os dias.
    c   Eu [estar] _____ tomando banho quando ele telefonou.

    d   Eles [**sentir-se**] _____ cansados depois de trabalhar todo o dia.

    e   Ela só [**querer**] _____ comprar uma coisa – uma blusa amarela!

    f   Antigamente, ele [**ir**] _____ ao cinema cada semana.

4 Choose the correct form of **ter**, and form the past participle of the verbs in bold, to form sentences using the pluperfect tense.

a	Maria e Lû	tinha	**ir** ao cinema quando eu cheguei.
b	Eu	tinha	**comprar** um novo carro.
c	O professor	tinha	**falar** muito antes de terminar
		tinham	a aula.
d	Eu e José	tínhamos	**comer** pouco.
e	Sra Guedes	tinham	**subir** ao quarto quando o marido telefonou.
f	Vocês		**viver** na França.

5 Change the verbs in **bold** into the present subjunctive.

    a   Espero que você **ter** uma boa viagem.
    b   Ana quer que o filho **estudar** bem.
    c   Talvez ela **fazer** um bolo delicioso.
    d   Duvidamos que vocês **abrir** seus livros hoje.
    e   É estranho que eles não **ir** à escola.
    f   Talvez nós não **falar** muito bem.

6 Write the answers to these sums in full in Portuguese.

    a $53 + 72 =$ _____
    b $14 + 9 =$ _____
    c $180 - 25 =$ _____
    d $250 \div 5 =$ _____
    e $46 + 362 =$ _____
    f $841 + 659 =$ _____
    g $1200 \div 20 =$ _____
    h $5 \times 500 =$ _____
    i $25{,}364 - 63 =$ _____
    j $123{,}801 + 99 =$ _____

7 Are the following numbers written correctly in Portuguese? If they are not, give the correct form in full.

✓/✗   correct version

a   531 = quinhentos e trinta e um ☐ _____
b   1,250 = mil, duzentos e cinqüenta ☐ _____
c   348 = trezentos e quarenta e nove ☐ _____
d   96 = noventa e seis ☐ _____
e   5,221 = cinco mil, duzentos e ☐ _____
       trinta e um
f   26,860 = vinte e seis mil, ☐ _____
       novecentos e sessenta
g   72 = setenta e dois ☐ _____
h   28 = vinte e oito ☐ _____

8 Choose the appropriate past participle from the box for each sentence to form a passive. Make it agree with the noun/pronoun.

a   O gato foi _____ pelo cão.
b   A porta foi _____ .
c   Eles foram _____ pelos soldados.
d   O carro foi _____ .
e   As casas foram _____ pelo terremoto (*earthquake*).
f   Eu (fem.) fui _____ .

| morto |
| decepcionado |
| vendido |
| mordido |
| destruído |
| aberto |

9 Can you find ten items of food or drink in this wordsearch?

O	B	M	E	Y	O	K	G	S	L
T	S	A	N	D	U	Í	C	H	E
N	O	L	E	I	T	E	Y	O	G
U	P	J	F	A	R	U	P	J	U
S	A	C	N	V	M	Ã	C	N	M
E	Y	O	E	Y	O	K	G	S	E
R	O	J	I	E	U	Q	R	U	S
P	A	Ç	Ú	C	A	R	U	P	J
F	A	C	N	W	T	I	L	H	D
Z	V	M	Q	R	O	H	N	I	V

10 Follow the numerical guidance, and fill in ten months of the year on the grid.

Across: 1 o décimo-primeiro mês
2 o quinto mês
3 o segundo
4 o quarto
5 o décimo-segundo
6 o sétimo

Down: 7 o primeiro mês
8 o nono mês
9 o terceiro
10 o décimo

11 Find the opposite pairs.

a	alto	i	magro
b	gordo	ii	chato
c	velho	iii	feio
d	interessante	iv	horrível
e	simpático	v	baixo
f	bonito	vi	jovem

12 Can you find ten parts of the body in this wordsearch?

O	L	H	O	K	G	S	M	Ã	O
K	G	S	X	B	Q	R	U	P	J
F	A	C	N	Q	D	O	K	G	S
X	B	C	A	B	E	Ç	A	C	N
A	C	N	O	K	D	A	C	N	P
N	W	C	N	R	O	R	U	P	É
R	A	C	N	W	E	B	Q	R	U
E	Y	R	U	P	J	L	H	D	Z
P	J	F	I	L	H	D	H	D	Z
V	M	E	Y	Z	V	M	E	A	C

taking it further

A selection of information on further reading, websites, and things connected with Brazilian Portuguese.

Reading

História da língua portuguesa, Paul Teyssier (Sá da Costa, 1990)
The Romance Languages, Martin Harris and Nigel Vincent (Routledge, 1997)
The Loom of Language, Frederick Bodmer (Allen & Unwin, 1946)
Dicionário Editora da língua portuguesa, good monolingual dictionary (new edn 1994)
Oxford–Duden pictorial dictionary, detail visual/vocabulary (1992)
Michaelis dicionário práctico, bilingual (English–Portuguese, both directions)
Collins Portuguese dictionaries, various sizes
In Action CD-ROM (Brazilian), Linguaphone
Brazil: The Once and Future Country, M. C. Eakin (St Martin's, 1997)
Lonely Planet Brazilian Phrase Book, M. Balla (Lonely Planet, 1990)

Learning

BBC series *Talk Portuguese*, 2003, includes one programme in Brazil. Also, *Brazil Inside Out*, 2003, a five-programme documentary series, with interviews with local people in five Brazilian regions.

Satellite TV, if you have access to it, will be able to reach Portuguese TV; there is an international channel called RTPi, which often features Brazilian **telenovelas**, or soap operas.

On-line courses, such as that offered by the University of Glasgow (UK), called *De tudo um pouco*.

Various Portuguese-learning CD-ROMs now available from good bookstores.

Enrol in language classes at your local college/language school.

Try to speak with the Brazilians when you are in Brazil – they will be grateful you have made an effort, and will encourage your attempts.

Websites

There are many sites and materials in both English and Portuguese. Here are just a few ideas:

Brazil on the web (Brazilian Embassy site): www.brazil.org.uk

Comunidade de Países de Língua Portuguesa – Portuguese-speaking communities: www.cplp.org

The human languages page – materials, interesting links, institutions and information in the language of your choice: www.june29.com

King's College, London – Dept. of Portuguese and Brazilian studies, various links: www.Kcl.ac.uk/depsta/humanities/pobrst/kclhp.htm

Língua Portuguesa – key this into any search engine (Altavista, Google, etc.) and you should link to many more sites.

Grant & Cutler – stockists of Portuguese books in the UK: www.grant-c.demon.co.uk

Portuguese pages linked to Amazon site: www.mediabooks.com

Universidade de Brasília: http://www.uub.br

Universidade de S. Paulo: http://www.usp.br

Art and culture: www.insite.com.br/art

Veja magazine: www.veja.com.br

Brazilian cinema: www.cinemabrasil.org.br

Unit 1

True or false?

a F b F c V

Exercise 1

1 b 2 b 3 a

Exercise 2

a Boa, Bem, b é c muito

Practice

1 a bom dia/boa tarde/boa noite (tarde) b obrigado/a, tchau
c sou/meu nome é X d Tem um apartamento reservado em
meu nome? e Oi, tudo bem? 2 Aqui está. / Sim, sou. /
Oito dias. / Tchau (adeus) 3 a sete b catorze c dezessete
d onze e treze 4 i dezoito 18 ii dez 10 5 a ii b iv c i
d iii e v 6 a John Harris b Liverpool c 6 days d room 12

Do you understand?

1 male 2 false 3 true 4 en-suite (5) false

Unit 2

True or false 1?

a f b f c v d f e v

True or false 2?

a f b f c v

Practice

1 Não, sou de Birmingham. / É grande e industrial. / Sim,
tenho um filho. / Ele se chama David. Tem 28 anos e é

professor de francês. / Sim, trabalho numa empresa
internacional.   **2**   **a** iii **b** v **c** i **d** ii **e** iv   **3**   1 a 2 b 3 b
4 a   **4**   **a** cinco/pequenas **b** brasileira **c** filhos interessantes
d histórica **e** dois vinhos alemães

Do you understand?

1 22 years old **2** very big, modern, very interesting, **3** no
4 language student, school secretary
5 Olá, John, Tudo bem? Eu estou muito bem. Vou te dizer um
pouco sobre quem sou. Meu nome é Gary, tenho dezenove
anos e sou de Bristol. É uma cidade muito bonita – histórica,
e turística. Sou casado e tenho um filho, Robert. Sou estudante
de tecnologia. Tchau, Gary.

Unit 3

True or false?

a f b v c v d v e f

Exercise

a sim b não c não

Practice

1   **a** é **b** são **c** está **d** é **e** sou/sou   **2**   Não, sou de Brighton.
/ É uma cidade pequena ao sul de Inglaterra. / Sim é bastante
perto.   **3**   **a** i **b** ii **c** ii
d iii **e** iii   **4**   1 Santos 2 Cantanduva 3 Campinas 4 Piracicaba
5 Uberaba

Do you understand?

1 f 2 f 3 v 4 f

Unit 4

Exercise 1

a no b yes c no

True or false?

a v b f c f

Exercise 2

1 b 2 a 3 a

Practice

1   **a** Há um açougue por aqui? **b** Onde há um correio? **c** Que
horas são? **d** São 2 e meia. **e** Na Alemanha chove (um) pouco.

2   **a** iii **b** i **c** iv **d** ii **e** v   3   **a** farmácia **b** mercado **c** café Silvana **d** praça D. Pedro   4   **a** Mexico **b** Japan **c** Brazil **d** France **e** England   5   Desculpe, sabe se há um mercado por aqui? / Sabe se está aberto agora? / São dez e um quarto (quinze). / Fica longe? / Obrigado/a, adeus (tchau).
6   **a** fica **b** ali **c** aqueles **d** terceira **e** para

Do you understand?

1 post office 2 Gomes Sá Street 3 Nascimento Street 4 4pm. 5 no

Unit 5

Exercise 1

a grande **b** num café **c** muito

Exercise 2

a f **b** v **c** f

Practice

1   **a** saio de casa **b** começo o trabalho **c** 12.45 **d** 1.30 **e** 18.05
2   **a** às sete e meia **b** às quinze para às nove **c** às duas e meia **d** às quatro e 25 **e** à uma e quinze **f** às dez para às oito
3   **a** Portugal é a seiscentos km da França. **b** O Brasil é a mil, oitocentos e noventa e seis km do México. **c** A Inglaterra é a mil, duzentos e quarenta e sete km de Portugal. **d** Os Estados Unidos são a seis mil, cento e vinte e cinco km da Argentina.
4   **a** iii **b** i **c** v **d** ii **e** iv

Do you understand?

1 true 2 Portuguese 3 D 4 A 5 false 6 E – airport

Unit 6

Exercise

a sports/TV **b** sports/TV
c reading/music

True or false?

a v **b** f **c** v

Practice

1   **a** ii **b** v **c** i **d** iv **e** iii   2   **a** conheço **b** sabe **c** sei **d** conhece **e** conhecem   3   Speaker 1=C, 2=A, 3=B   4   Adoro nadar,

vou à piscina aos sábados. / Sim, um pouco. / Prefiro a música jazz. Francisco, o que você faz no tempo livre? / Também gosto do teatro, mas os ingressos são bastante caros.

Do you understand?

1   Vinhos / Mary Black / High Street, no. 10 / CEP 23410 Centro / Southampton Hants.   2   **a** violão **b** mecânica geral **c** desenho artístico e publicitário

Unit 7

Exercise 1

C

Exercise 2

a sapatos **b** 39 **c** R85

Practice

1   **a** ii **b** iii **c** i **d** vi **e** v
2   Tem saias? / Acho que é o 42. / Tem em azul-claro? / Quanto é, (custa)? / Levo esta em azul e aquela em preto. / Obrigada   3   **a** compre / Buy the blouse! **b** comam / Eat the bread! **c** vão / Go through (by) here! **d** faça / Don't be noisy! **e** trabalhe / Work hard! **f** falem / Don't talk a lot!
4   **a** boots **b** 39 **c** brown **d** too big **e** R$98

Do you understand?

1 salads 2 eat fruits, not sweet things, 3 make a dinner 4 have a good salt bath 5 relax a lot 6 massage

Unit 8

Exercise 1

a v **b** f **c** f

Exercise 2

a yes **b** no **c** yes

Practice

1   **a** Tem uma mesa livre? **b** Somos cinco. **c** Não tenho sede. **d** Que vai pedir? **e** Garçom por favor. **f** A conta por favor.
2   **a** sigam **b** faça **c** beba **d** repitam **e** falem **f** traga   3   Para começar uma sopa de legumes. / Ovelha com arroz e salada. / Uma cerveja e uma jarra de água.   4   sobremesa / hoje / sorvete / baunilha / avelã / sim   5   **a** tenho fome **b** tem calor

c temos sono **d** tem frio **e** têm sede **6** **a** iii **b** ii **c** i **d** iv
7 **a** dessert **b** drink **c** drink **d** starter **e** main meal **f** side dish **g** starter **h** side dish

Do you understand?

Laura – creme de aspargos, omelete, fruta. Marcelo – canja, frango, doce de côco. Sérgio – lula frita, espeto misto, pudim de caramelo. You – no starter, bife na brasa, sorvete. Rita – canja, peixe, fruta.

Unit 9

Practice

1 **a** meus **b** sua/ a amiga dele **c** nossa **d** suas/ as irmãs delas **e** sua **2** **a** Pode me levar ao centro da cidade? **b** Boa viagem! **c** A que horas parte o próximo ônibus (de luxo) para o Rio? **d** Tem troco para uma nota de R$50? **e** O que faço para chegar na praça Miraflores? **f** Conhece um bom restaurante aqui?
3 A que horas parte o próximo ônibus para Fortaleza? / Queria um bilhete de ida e volta. / Tem troco para uma nota de R$100? / O ônibus sai de onde?
4 **a** iv **b** i **c** v **d** iii **e** ii
5 c/f/a/d/g/b/e/h

Do you understand?

1 T 2 F 3 F

Unit 10

Exercise 1

a R$360 **b** no **c** no

Exercise 2

Any 3 of: air-conditioning not working / tap won't close / pillow dirty / blinds don't open properly

Practice

1 Bom dia, tem um apartamento livre? / Simples por favor. Com banheiro. / Para três dias. / Quanto é por noite? / (Está bem). Onde fica o apartamento? **2** **a** iii **b** i **c** v **d** iv **e** ii or iii **f** i **g** i **3** Twin/ with bathroom/3/Saturday/ 135/R$38 per person **4** **a** Desculpe, o garfo está sujo. **b** ... o ar-condicionado não está funcionando. **c** ... a torneira está pingando. **d** ... o prato está partido. **e** ... falta uma colher.
5 **a** ir **b** comer **c** terminar **d** ver **e** beber

Do you understand?

1 Napoli 2 credit card 3 I double 4 fridge 5 Silvini 6 38 7 none
8 breakfast and dinner

Unit 11
Practice

1   a odeia a rede b não gosto dos cachimbos c preferimos a
cerâmica d gosta dos brincos e adoram os artigos de couro
2   a mim b deles c nela d si e você   3   a 1 b 2 c 1 d 2 e 2
4   Estou procurando presentes para minha família. / Tem
uma rede? / Quanto é? / Que tem para senhoras? / Vou levar a
rede, e esta tapeçaria.

Do you understand?

1 17 2 from next year 3 40 4 school 5 guaraná and other soft
drinks 6 a) coelhinho, b quadrinhos, c aulas

Unit 12
Exercise

 a Aliens b não c satírica d tarde e táxi

Practice

1   a Por que não vamos ao museu? b A que horas começa o
filme? c O concerto termina às dez e meia d Que boa
exposição! e Você é meu convidado João f Voltamos de
ônibus?   2   a eu me b lhe c te d ele e lo   3   a ii b i c ii
d Star Wars e 8.30 f i   4   Por que não vamos almoçar
naquele barzinho ali? / Venha, eu te convido e sou eu quem pago.
/ Insisto, você é meu/minha convidado/a. / Vamos.   5   a no
avião da b trem das 2 horas c de táxi/a pé d no carro de

Do you understand?

Film A=iii / B=i / C=ii a A b B
c Vietnam d both e 2 f autobiography

Unit 13
True or false?

a f b f c v d f

Practice

1 Boa tarde, quanto custa enviar este pacote a Alemanha por favor? / Bom, queria enviar o pacote e também queria dez selos. / Não, três para Espanha e sete para Inglaterra. / Obrigado/a, onde é a caixa? **2** Buys: ovos / biscoitos / presunto / cerveja / pãezinhos. / Not available: açúcar/mel. / Extra item: olive oil – azeite. **3** **a** este **b** essa **c** aqueles **d** estes **e** essas **4** As per tape **5** **a** Eu posso alugar um carro aqui? **b** É para oito dias, começando de hoje. **c** O que faço para chegar no Rio? **d** Parece que estou perdido/a. **e** Ponha doze litros de álcool por favor. **f** Pode verificar a água para mim? **6** **a** aberto or fechado **b** abertas or fechadas **c** feitos **d** paga **e** escrita **7** unleaded / 18 litres / no / R$11 **8** Bom dia / proibido / praça / perdida / Rio / direita / sinais / segunda / esquerda / estrada

Do you understand?

a ii **b** i **c** iv **d** xii **e** viii **f** v **g** ix **h** vi **i** x **j** xi **k** iii **l** vii

Unit 14

Practice

1 **a** Que vai fazer quarta feira à tarde Paul? **b** Estarei lá às dez e meia. **c** Por que não vamos nadar? **d** A que horas nos encontramos? **e** Estou livre a partir das quatro e quinze. **f** Alô, quem fala? **2** **a** Carlos Silves **b** Banco do Brasil **c** Thurs a.m. **d** French lesson **e** golf **f** 11.45 **g** hospital **3** Examples: **a** Amanhã eu comprarei um carro. **b** O mês que vem nós visitaremos Alemanha. **c** No domingo Cristina fará um bolo. **d** O próximo ano eles ganharão a loteria. **e** Depois de amanhã a Sra Lopes escreverá uma carta. **4** **a** eles estão dormindo **b** ela está comendo **c** nós estamos estudando **d** eu estou andando **e** elas estão falando **5** **a** f **b** v **c** v **d** f **e** f **f** v **6** **a** vi **b** iii **c** i **d** ii **e** iv **f** v

Do you understand?

a novembro **b** festas **c** flores **d** Estados Unidos **e** ano **f** cores **1** nature **2** roses, plants, flowers, **3** new varieties of rose, 15 different colours of petunia **4** 1954

Unit 15

Exercise

1 c **2** a **3** b

Practice

1 a Visitou o museu? **b** Ficamos duas semanas na Itália. **c** Quando voltaram de Nova Iorque? **d** Tem algum recado para mim? **e** Acabo de chegar no hotel. **f** Os italianos falam tão rapidamente.   **2   a** comi **b** compraram **c** partimos **d** gostaram **e** escreveu   **3   a** viu **b** fiz **c** pusemos **d** foram **e** teve **4** Voltei ontem à tarde. Cheguei aqui às três e vinte e cinco. / Sim, muito. Andei na praia em Copacabana, visitei o Pão de Açúcar e vi as favelas. / Sim, comi feijoada e provei a caipirinha.   **5   a** Eles se levantaram cedo. **b** Ela correu rapidamente. **c** Elas cantaram mal. **d** Nós falamos devagar. **e** Eu toquei piano bem.   **6**   Inglaterra/ teatro/ visitei/ palácio/ Grécia/ gregos/ interessantes/ dança/ São Paulo/ 5 dias/ Brasília

Do you understand?

1 Estados Unidos. **2** Muito quente. **3** Michael Jackson e atores. **4** Não muito saudável. **5** Discoteca. **6** Falta de guaraná. **7** Sábado.

Unit 16

Exercise

a dois quadros **b** feira-hippy **c** pedras preciosas

Practice

1   a todas as semanas **b** todos os anos **c** todos os ... custam **d** todos os dias **e** todas as pessoas ganham **f** todos os meses **2**   Comprei-o (o comprei) na feira-hippy na praça. / Não muito. Só 42 reais. Gosta? / Comprou alguma coisa? / Que livro mais interessante!   **3   a** carro nosso **b** estas botas minhas **c** este gato de José **d** esta casa sua **e** estes livros deles **4   1** went to Spain   **2** years ago **2** visited Taj Mahal **3** months ago **3** had lunch ½ hour ago **4** went to cinema **5** days ago

Do you understand?

1 umbrella **2** restaurant Mineiro **3** 20 minutes ago **4** company name **5** shop doorway

Unit 17

Practice

1   a Havia uma blusa na vitrine de que gostei. **b** Estava à direita da vitrine. **c** Ela era baixa, tinha cabelo comprido e

olhos azuis. **d** Ele tinha provavelmente 40 e tantos anos. **e** Não é mais interessante hoje em dia? **f** Nadávamos todos os dias.
2 **a** fui **b** era **c** jantávamos **d** comiam **e** veio **f** estava
3 Body i = dress, long hair ii = t-shirt, skirt, short hair, glasses iii = hat, moustache, shirt, trousers **4** **a** íamos ii **b** brincávamos iv **c** tínhamos i **d** estudávamos v **e** passávamos iii **5** Havia uma camisa na vitrine, mas já não está mais lá. / Era preta e feita de lã. / Estava à esquerda da vitrine detrás das calças. / Não obrigado/a. Só queria aquela. **6** **a** iii **b** ii **c** i **d** iv

Do you understand?

1 era 2 defendia 3 brigava 4 cheguei 5 criei 6 estavam 7 achei 8 consegui 9 veio 10 começamos a t b t c f d f e t f f

Unit 18

True or false?

a v b f c f

Practice

1 **a** Não me sinto nada bem. **b** Onde dói? **c** Tem alguma coisa para dor dos dentes? **d** (O) que tem para enxaquecas? **e** Que aconteceu? **f** Houve um acidente na rua Campo.
2 **a** iii **b** iv **c** v **d** vi **e** ii **f** i **3** **a** iii melhore **b** iv esteja **c** i estudem **d** vi venha **e** ii ganhemos **f** v ame **4** D Pedro square / 2 / broken arm, cut leg / corner with Main Street / Alexandra Esteves **5** **a** estava fechada **b** foram dados pelo dono **c** estavam abertas **d** fui convidado/a **e** foi escrita por Luís **f** estavam sujos **6** Tem alguma coisa para dor de cabeça? / Levo as aspirinas. / Não, que tem para alergias? / Levo um frasco do creme. Quanto é por favor? Obrigado/a, adeus.

Revision Unit 1

1   o/a/as/o/os uma/uns/umas/um/uma   2   a este b essa
c Aqueles d destas e Esses f Aquela or Esta   3   a Tudo
b Todas c todo d toda e tudo f Todas   4   a trinta e seis
b cento e cinqüenta e dois c quinhentos d mil, trezentos e
vinte e um e cinco mil e oitocentos f doze mil, seiscentos e
cinqüenta e quatro g vinte e cinco mil, novecentos e noventa
e nove h cem mil i catorze j noventa e cinco   5   a 899
b 723 c 468 d 2,501 e 4,802 f 7,554 g 11,100 h 68,336 i 105
j 307   6   a comem b falo c vai d parte e fazemos f viaja
g escrevem h compreendem   7   a é b está c é/fica d estão
e são/ficam f são g é/fica h é   8   a tem   ii b há   vii c
temos   viii d há   iii e tenho   vi f têm   i g tem   iv h há
v   9   a Fale b coma c Feche d abram e Bebam f subam
g comece h Preencha   10   1 americanos 2 Inglaterra
3 espanhol 4 Brasil 5 França 6 alemães 7 gregos 8 Itália
9 chinês 10 Alemanha   11   a vestido b saia c calças
d sapato e camisa f blusa g chapéu h luvas i casaco j gravata
12   vermelho/roxo/verde/azul/marrom/rosa/branco/
preto/amarelo   13   Across: 1 supermercado
2 banco 6 sapataria 7 mercado 8 quiosque Down:
3 correio 4 açougue 5 livraria 9 café 10 cinema.

Revision Unit 2

1   a subitamente b Finalmente c Imediatamente
d facilmente e Aparentemente f temporariamente g mal
2   a compreenderam b partiram c vendi d chegaram
e esteve f perceberam g teve h Tiramos   3   a tinha
b acordávamos c estava d sentiam-se e queria f ia
4   a tinham ido b tinha comprado c tinha falado

d tínhamos comido **e** tinha subido **f** tinham vivido
5   **a** tenha **b** estude **c** faça **d** abram **e** vão **f** falemos
6   **a** Cento e vinte e cinco **b** Vinte e três **c** Cento e cinqüenta e
cinco **d** Cinqüenta **e** Quatrocentos e oito **f** Mil e quinhentos
g Sessenta **h** Dois mil e quinhentos **i** Vinte e cinco mil,
trezentos e um **j** Cento e vinte e três mil e novecentos
7   **a** ✓ **b** ✓ **c** ✗ trezentos e quarenta e oito **d** ✓ **e** ✗ cinco mil,
duzentos e vinte e um **f** ✗ vinte e seis mil, oitocentos e sessenta
g ✓ **h** ✓   **8**   **a** mordido **b** aberta **c** mortos **d** vendido
e destruídas **f** decepcionada   **9**   sopa/pão/vinho/açúcar/legumes/
sanduíche/presunto/queijo/ cerveja/leite   **10**   **1** novembro
2 maio **3** fevereiro **4** abril **5** dezembro **6** julho **7** janeiro
8 setembro **9** março **10** outubro   **11**   **a** v **b** i **c** vi **d** ii **e** iv **f** iii
12   braço/perna/cabeça/mão/olho dedo/boca/pé/orelha/nariz

accents These are written marks above letters which affect either how that letter is pronounced, or at what point the word should be stressed (emphasized) when spoken. An accent can also be used to differentiate between two words with identical spellings but with different meanings. English does not use written accents (apart from on foreign words imported into the language), but many other languages do: e.g. *câmbio, fantástico; por = by/for pôr = to put*

adjectives Words which describe, or give more information about, nouns. In Portuguese, adjectives match their endings to the nouns they are linked with (e.g. if they are singular/plural or masculine/feminine): e.g. *a cold cup of tea / that expensive coat um chá frio / aquele casaco caro.*

adverbs These are words which describe, or tell us more about, how an action (verb) is being carried out. They often answer the question HOW? They are also used to describe adjectives more fully, and you can use two adverbs together too. Often in English, an adverb has the ending '-ly' on it: e.g. *He sings loudly. / They ran incredibly quickly. Canta altamente. / Correram incrivelmente rapidamente.*

articles Words which go with nouns – definite articles are the words for 'the', and indefinite articles are the words for 'a/an/some'. In Portuguese there are different words corresponding to the number and gender (masculine/feminine): *o/a/os/as* (definite) and *um/uma/ uns/umas* (indefinite).

clause A group of words which also contains a verb: e.g. *before we go out ... / if she swims well ... antes de sairmos ... / se ela nada bem ...*

comparative Forms of adjectives and adverbs used to make comparisons, e.g. *fatter / more slowly mais gordo / mais devagar.*

demonstratives The words used for pointing things out – this / that / these / those *este / esse / aquele / estes* etc.

imperative A form of verb, known as a mood, used when giving commands: *Eat your dinner! Come o jantar!*

infinitive The part of the verb referred to in English as 'To ...', and the form found in the dictionary before you change any of its endings: to *speak* / to *drink* / to *leave falar / beber / partir.*

interrogatives Question forms, e.g. *where/ / which? onde? / qual?*

nouns A noun is any thing, person or abstract idea in existence – everything around us is a noun of some kind. A noun can be singular (just one), or plural (more than one). In Portuguese nouns are also divided into masculine and feminine words: e.g. *table / horses / man–men / happiness mesa / cavalos / homem–homens / felicidade.*

number Whether a word is singular (just one), or plural (more than one).

object The person or thing on the receiving end of the action of a verb. Objects can be 'direct' – i.e. they dirctly receive the action of the verb – or 'indirect' – where they receive the results of the action, through indirect means: e.g. *She gives money every week* ('money' is direct object) / *she gives them money every week.* ('them' is indirect object) *Dá dinheiro todas as semanas. / Dá-lhes dinheiro ... .*

phrase A group of words which together have some meaning: e.g. *in the square / after mid-day na praça / depois de meio-dia*

possessives Words showing ownership or possession, e.g. *my car / it's ours o meu carro / é nosso.*

prefix A number of letters which may be added to the beginning of a word, which change its meaning in some way: e.g. *possible – impossible / possível – impossível.*

prepositions These are words which denote the 'position' of someone or something in time or place: e.g. *on top of the cupboard / before going out / at six o'clock em cima do armário / antes de sair / às seis horas.*

pronouns These are words which take the place of a noun (*pro* = for), so that you do not need to keep repeating the actual noun itself each time you want to refer to it. There are various types of pronoun, all of which you will learn about in Portuguese: e.g. *Maria is very kind. She looks after my cat. She gives it lots of treats. (A) Maria / Ela / -o.*

reflexive verbs Actions with a bearing on the subject of the verb – actions are carried out by, and also on, the subject, i.e. they 'reflect' back to the person carrying out the action. In English reflexive verbs carry the word 'self' with them. A number of verbs in Portuguese are reflexive where you would not expect them to be in English: e.g. *Enjoy yourselves! / She gets herself dressed each morning. Divertam-se! / Veste-se cada manhã.*

sentence A group of words, with a beginning, an end, and a finite verb (see below), which has a meaning. A sentence may have any number of separate clauses, but one of these will be the main clause, which can make sense in its own right as a sentence: e.g. *She wants to visit America. / If you go there, you must not drink the water. Ela quer visitar os Estados Unidos. / Se for lá, não deveria beber a água.*

subject The person or thing carrying out the action of a verb: e.g. *My brother wants to be a teacher. / Our dog always chases spiders. O meu irmão ... / O nosso cachorro ...*

subjunctive mood A separate set of verb endings for use in certain situations, such as in 'if' clauses, or with expressions of doubt: e.g. *I doubt he's coming Duvido que ele venha.*

suffix A number of letters which may be added to the end of a word, which change the meaning or the type of grammatical word it is: e.g. *sad – sadness / glad – gladly triste – tristeza / feliz – felizmente.*

superlative The form of an adjective or adverb denoting the highest or lowest level, e.g. *the fastest car / the cheapest shoes o carro mais rápido / os sapatos mais baratos.*

syllable This is a part of a word containing one, two, or more letters which are clumped together so that we can divide up the word as we say it: e.g. *cho-co-late / mag-ni-fi-cent cho-co-la-te / mag-ní-fi-co.*

tenses These are the time references for when verbs are taking place. There are different tenses in the present, past and future – you will learn what these are in Portuguese. Some of them have different names in Portuguese grammar to what they might be termed in English – don't worry too much about the actual terminology; concentrate on learning which verb endings to use in what circumstances: e.g. *She had not wanted to go to the party. / Will we have saved enough money? Não tinha querido ir à festa. / Teremos poupado dinheiro suficiente?*

verbs Verbs convey actions of states of being, or sometimes abstract states. Verbs have an 'infinitive' form, which tells you the name of the verb itself, but no other information – it is the form you will find in the dictionary, and relates to the English 'TO do something'. A sentence must have a verb in a 'finite' form – which tells you what the action is, who is doing it, and at what point in time (in the past, present or future). English does not change many of its verb endings, but Portuguese, as many languages, has different endings for the person doing the action, and the time, or tense: e.g. *She goes home at 5 o'clock.* / *I watched TV last night.* **Ela volta para casa às cinco.** / **Vi a televisão ontem à noite.**

um (uma)	1	vinte e um (uma)	21
dois (duas)	2	trinta	30
três	3	quarenta	40
quatro	4	cinqüenta	50
cinco	5	sessenta	60
seis	6	setenta	70
sete	7	oitenta	80
oito	8	noventa	90
nove	9	cem (cento)	100
dez	10	cento e um (uma)	101
onze	11	duzentos/as	200
doze	12	trezentos/as	300
treze	13	quatrocentos/as	400
catorze, quatorze	14	quinhentos/as	500
quinze	15	seiscentos/as	600
dezesseis	16	setecentos/as	700
dezessete	17	oitocentos/as	800
dezoito	18	novecentos/as	900
dezenove	19	mil	1 000
vinte	20	um milhão	1 000 000

primeiro/a, 1º/1ª	*first*	sexto/a	*sixth*
segundo/a, 2º/2ª	*second*	sétimo/a	*seventh*
terceiro/a, 3º/3ª	*third*	oitavo/a	*eighth*
quarto/a, 4º/4ª	*fourth*	nono/a	*ninth*
quinto/a, 5º/5ª	*fifth*	décimo/a	*tenth*

BP–English vocabulary

à direita *on the right*
à esquerda *on the left*
a pé *on foot*
abafado *close, hot*
aberto *open*
advogado/a *lawyer*
aeroporto (o) *airport*
agenda (a) *diary*
agora *now*
aguardente (o) *firewater*
álcool (o) *alcohol*
alô *hello*
amigos (os) *friends*
andar (o) *floor*
anos (os) *years*
antigo/a *old*
ao fundo *at the back*
ao lado de *next to*
aos sábados *on Saturdays*
apartamento (o) *room*
aquele/aquela *that*
aqui *here*
arroz com marisco (o) *seafood rice*
às vezes *sometimes*
aspirina (a) *aspirin*
até *until, up to*
avenida (a) *avenue*
avião (o) *aeroplane*
azeite (o) *olive oil*

banco (o) *bank*
banheiro (o) *bathroom*
barco (o) *boat*
barulhento/a *noisy*
bastante *quite*
bem *well*

bem-vindo/a *welcome*
bicicleta (a) *bicycle*
bilhete (o) *ticket*
blusa (a) *blouse*
bolsa (a) *bag*
bom *good, right then*
bonito *pretty*
botas (as) *boots*

cá *here*
cada ... *every ...*
café (o) *café/coffee*
café da manhã *breakfast*
caixa (a) *cash desk, till*
calças (as) *trousers*
cama (a) *bed*
camisa (a) *shirt*
canja (a) *chicken broth*
capoeira (a) *acrobatic dance*
cardápio (o) *menu*
carne (a) *meat*
caro *expensive*
carro (o) *car*
carteira (a) *wallet, purse*
casa (a) *house*
casado/a *married*
casal *couple, double*
cataratas (as) *waterfalls*
cavalo (o) *horse*
cedo *early*
centro (o) *centre*
chamo-me/me chamo *my name is*
chave (a) *key*
chega *arrives*
chope (o) *lager*
chuva (a) *rain*

cidade (a) *town, city*
clube (o) *social club*
coisa (a) *thing*
com *with*
come *s/he eats*
comemos *we eat*
comida (a) *food*
como é? *what is it like?*
comprar *to buy*
comprimido (o) *pill*
conhecer *to get to know*
contra *against*
cor (a) *colour*
correio (o) *post office*
couro (o) *leather*
cultura (a) *culture*
cultural *cultural*
custa *it costs*

daqui *from here*
de nada *don't mention it*
de onde é? *where are you from?*
de onde são? *where are you from?*
   (pl.)
de vez em quando *sometimes*
debaixo de *underneath*
deixar *to leave*
delicioso/a *delicious*
dentro *inside*
depois *then, after*
desculpe *excuse me*
dia (o) *day*
detrás de *behind*
difícil *difficult*
dinheiro (o) *money*
diz *s/he says*
durante *during*
dúzia (a) *dozen*

e *and*
é *is*
em *in, on*
em frente de *in front of*
em geral *generally*
empresa (a) *business, company*
encher *to fill*
endereço (o) *address*
enorme *enormous*
então *well then*
entre *in between*
escola (a) *school*

escritório (o) *office*
Espanha (a) *Spain*
espanhois *Spanish* (pl.)
esquina (a) *corner*
está bem *O.K.*
estação (a) *station*
este/esta *this*
estilo (o) *style*
estou bem *I'm well*
estrada (a) *highway*
estudante *student*
eu *I*

fala? *do you speak?*
falo *I speak*
família (a) *family*
faça favor de ... *please ...*
farmácia (a) *chemist's*
feijoada (a) *bean stew*
férias (as) *holidays*
fica *is situated*
ficar *to stay/be situated*
ficha (a) *form*
filha (a) *daughter*
filho (o) *son*
flores (as) *flowers*
fome (a) *hunger*
fora *outside*
França (a) *France*
frango (o) *chicken*
funcionar *to work*

garrafa (a) *bottle*
gasóleo (o) *diesel*
gasolina (a) *petrol*
gato (o) *cat*
gaúcho (o) *cowboy*
gente (a) *people*
gentil *kind*
geralmente *generally*
gosta/am? *do you like?*
gostam *they like*
gostamos *we like*
gostaria de *I would like to*
gosto *I like*
graças a Deus *thank goodness*
grande *big*
Grécia (a) *Greece*

há *there is, are*
há meia hora *½ hour ago*

havia *there was, were*
histórico *historical*
hoje *today*
hotel (o) *hotel*

ida e volta *return (ticket)*
ida (a) *single (ticket)*
idade (a) *age*
igualmente *likewise*
incluindo *including*
índios (os) *indians*
informações *information*
inglês/esa *English*
internacional *international*
interessante *interesting*
ir *to go*
irmã (a) *sister*
irmão (o) *brother*
isso *that's it*

jacaré (o) *alligator*
Japão (o) *Japan*
jogar *to play*
jornais (os) *newspapers*

lá, ali *there*
lamento *I'm sorry*
laranjas (as) *oranges*
leio *I read*
leite (o) *milk*
ler *to read*
levo *I'll take*
limão (o) *lime*
limpo *clean*
lindo *pretty*
linha (a) *platform*
litoral *coastal*
litro (o) *litre*
livros (os) *books*
loja (a) *shop*
Londres *London*
longe *a long way*

mãe (a) *mother*
maior *bigger*
mais de *more than*
mais ou menos *more or less*
mais tarde *later*
mala (a) *suitcase*
manteiga (a) *butter*
mapa (o) *map*

maravilhoso *wonderful*
marido (o) *husband*
mariscos (os) *seafood*
mas *but*
médico/a *doctor*
meio quilo *half a kilo*
melhorar *to improve*
mês (o) *month*
mesa (a) *table*
mesmo ali *right there*
moderno *modern*
momento (o) *moment*
mora *live/s*
moram *they, you live*
moro *I live*
mosquitos (os) *mosquitoes*
movimentado *busy*
muitas vezes *often*
muito *very*
muito bem *very well*
muito prazer *pleased to meet you*
mulher (a) *wife*
mundo (o) *world*
museu (o) *museum*
música (a) *music*

na *in/on the*
nadar *to swim*
não *no*
não funciona *it doesn't work*
neve (a) *snow*
nome (o) *name*
número (o) *number*
nunca *never*

o que faz? *what do you do?*
obrigado/a *thank you*
óculos (os) *glasses*
óleo (o) *oil*
ônibus (o) *bus*
ontem *yesterday*
oportunidade (a) *opportunity*
outono (o) *Autumn*
ouço *I listen to*
outros (os) *(the) others*
ouvir *to listen to*
ovos (os) *eggs*

pacote (o) *packet*
pai (o) *father*
país (o) *country*

pais (os) *parents*
pão (o) *bread*
para *in order to/for*
para nós *for us*
parte *departs*
partido *broken*
passamos *we spend*
passaporte (o) *passport*
passar *to pass/spend*
pastelaria (a) *cake shop*
pedir *to ask for*
pegar *to get, catch*
pelo menos *at least*
pequeno/a *small*
pêras (as) *pears*
perto *near*
pessoalmente *personally*
picante *spicy*
pingar *to drip*
pintar *to paint*
piscina (a) *swimming pool*
plástico *plastic*
podem *you (pl.) can*
podemos *we can*
pois *well*
poluição (a) *pollution*
pôr *to put*
por noite *per night*
por favor *please*
porque *because*
porta (a) *door*
porto (o) *port*
português/esa *Portuguese*
posso? *may I?*
postal (o) *postcard*
pouquinho (um) *a little bit*
praça (a) *square*
preciso de *I need*
preço (o) *price*
preencher *to fill in*
prefere *he she, you prefer(s)*
preferem *they, you prefer*
preferimos *we prefer*
prefiro *I prefer*
presunto (o) *smoked ham*
primeiro *first*
problema (o) *problem*
professor *teacher*
provar *to try, taste*
provavelmente *probably*
próximo *nearby*

puxa! *goodness!*

quadro (o) *picture*
qual? *which?*
quanto é? *how much is it?*
quantos/as *how many?*
quarto (o) *1/4 litre bottle*
quarto (o) *bedroom*
que *that, which*
que mais? *what else?*
que tal? *how about?*
queijo (o) *cheese*
quem? *who?*
quente *hot*
quer *s/he wants*
quilo (o) *kilo*

rápido *fast*
recepção (a) *reception*
recomendo *I recommend*
refeições (as) *meals*
refeitório (o) *canteen*
refrigerante (o) *soft drink*
região (a) *region*
reservado *reserved*
reservar *to reserve*
revistas (as) *magazines*
roupas (as) *clothes*
rua (a) *road*

sabe? *do you know?*
saia (a) *skirt*
saída (a) *exit*
sanduíche (o) *sandwich*
sapatos (os) *shoes*
saudável *healthy*
saúde (a) *health*
se *if*
se Deus quiser *God willing*
selo (o) *stamp*
sem *without*
sempre *always*
senhores (os) *you*
sentar-se *to sit down*
sentir-se *to feel*
sim *yes*
sinais (os) *road signs*
sobremesa (a) *dessert*
sobrenome (o) *surname*
somos *we are*
sorvete (o) *ice cream*

sou *I am*
sou de *I am from*
sujo *dirty*
suco (o) *fruit juice*

tamanho (o) *size*
também *also*
tão *so*
tarde (a) *afternoon*
táxi (o) *taxi*
tchau *bye*
telenovelas (as) *soap-operas*
televisão (a) *television*
têm *they have*
tem ...? *do you have ...?*
temos *we have*
tempo (o) *time*
tempo de lazer (o) *leisure time*
tempo livre (o) *free time*
tenho *I have*
terceiro *third*
terra (a) *land, hometown*
tipicamente *typically*
típico *typical*
todas as noites *every night*
todos os dias *every day*
tomar *to take*
trabalha *you work*

trabalho *I work*
transeunte *passer-by*
trocar *to change*
tudo *everything*
tudo bem? *O.K.?*

um pouco *a bit*
um pouco de *a bit of*
universidade (a) *university*

vago *free*
vários/as *various*
velho/a *old*
vende *s/he sells*
vende-se/se vende *for sale*
vento (o) *wind*
ver *to see, watch*
verão (o) *summer*
vestido (o) *dress*
viagem (a) *journey*
vidro (o) *window, glass*
vinho (o) *wine*
vir *to come*
vista (a) *view*
vive *lives*

xarope (o) *syrup, remedy*

a bit (of) *um pouco (de)*
a long way *longe*
address *endereço (o)*
aeroplane *avião (o)*
afternoon *tarde (a)*
against *contra*
age *idade (a)*
aiport *aeroporto (o)*
alcohol *álcool (o)*
alligator *jacaré (o)*
also *também*
always *sempre*
and *e*
arrives *chega*
aspirin *aspirina (a)*
at least *pelo menos*
at the back *ao fundo*
autumn *outono (o)*
avenue *avenida (a)*

bag *bolsa (a)*
bank *banco (o)*
bathroom *banheiro (o)*
bean stew *feijoada (a)*
because *porque*
bed *cama (a)*
bedroom *quarto (o)*
behind *detrás de*
bicycle *bicicleta (a)*
big *grande*
bigger *maior (mais grande)*
blouse *blusa (a)*
boat *barco (o)*
books *livros (os)*
boots *botas (as)*
bottle *garrafa (a)*
bread *pão (o)*

breakfast *café da manhã (o)*
broken *partido*
brother *irmão (o)*
bus *ônibus (o)*
business, company *empresa (a)*
busy *movimentado, ocupado*
but *mas*
butter *manteiga (a)*
bye *tchau*

café/coffee *café (o)*
cake shop *pastelaria (a)*
canteen *cantina (a)*
car *carro, automóvel (o)*
cash desk, till *caixa (a)*
cat *gato (o)*
centre *centro (o)*
cheese *queijo (o)*
chemist's *farmácia (a)*
chicken *frango (o), galinha (a)*
chicken broth *canja (a)*
clean *limpo*
close, hot *abafado*
clothes *roupa (a)*
coastal *litoral*
colour *cor (a)*
corner *esquina (a)*
country *país (o)*
couple, double *casal (o)*
cowboy *gaúcho (o)*
cultural *cultural*
culture *cultura (a)*

daughter *filha (a)*
day *dia (o)*
delicious *delicioso*
departs *parte*

dessert *sobremesa (a)*
diary *agenda (a)*
diesel *gasóleo (o)*
difficult *difícil*
dirty *sujo*
do you know? *sabe?*
do you like? *gosta?*
do you speak? *fala?*
doctor *médico (o)*
don't mention it *de nada*
door *porta (a)*
dozen *dúzia (a)*
dress *vestido (o)*
during *durante*

early *cedo*
eggs *ovos (os)*
English *inglês*
enormous *enorme*
every *cada*
every day *cada dia/todos os dias*
every night *cada noite/todas as noites*
everything *tudo*
excuse me *desculpe*
exit *saída (a)*
expensive *caro*

family *família (a)*
fast *rápido*
father *pai (o)*
firewater *aguardente (o)*
first *primeiro*
floor *andar (o)*
flowers *flores (as)*
food *comida (a)*
for sale *vende-se*
form *ficha (a)*
France *França (a)*
free time *tempo livre (o)*
friends *amigos (os)*
from here *daqui*
fruit juice *suco (o)*

generally *geralmente*
glasses *óculos (os)*
God willing *se Deus quiser*
good, right then *bom*
goodness! *puxa!*
Greece *Grécia (a)*

half a kilo *meio quilo*
half an hour ago *há meia hora*

health *saúde (a)*
healthy *saudável*
hello *oi*
here *aqui, cá*
highway *estrada (a)*
historical *histórico*
holidays *férias (as)*
horse *cavalo (o)*
hot *quente*
hotel *hotel (o)*
house *casa (a)*
how about? *que tal?*
how many? *quantos?*
how much is it? *quanto é?*
hunger *fome (a)*
husband *marido (o)*

I am from *sou de*
I like *gosto (de)*
I would like to *gostaria (de)*
I'll take *levo*
I'm sorry *lamento/sinto muito*
I'm well *estou bem*
ice-cream *sorvete (o)*
if *se*
in between *entre*
in front of *em frente de*
in order to/for *para*
in, on *em*
in/on the *no, na*
including *incluindo, incluso*
information *informações (as)*
inside *dentro*
interesting *interessante*
international *internacional*
is situated *fica*
it costs *custa*
it doesn't work *não funciona*

Japan *Japão (o)*
journey *viagem (a)*

key *chave (a)*
kilo *quilo (o)*
kind *simpático*

lager *chope (o)*
land, hometown *terra (a)*
later *mais tarde*
lawyer *avogado (o)*
leather *couro (o)*
leisure time *tempo de lazer (o)*

lime *limão (o)/lima (a)*
litre *litro (o)*
live/s *mora*
London *Londres*

magazines *revistas (as)*
map *mapa (o)*
married *casado*
may I? *posso?*
meals *refeições (as)*
menu *cardápio (o)*
milk *leite (o)*
modern *moderno*
moment *momento (o)*
money *dinheiro (o)*
month *mês (o)*
more or less *mais ou menos*
more than *mais (de) que*
mosquitoes *mosquitos (os)*
mother *mãe (a)*
museum *museu (o)*
music *música (a)*
my name is ... *o meu nome é ...*

name *nome (o)*
near *perto*
never *nunca*
newspapers *jornais (os)*
next to *ao lado de*
no, not *não*
noisy *barulhento*
now *agora*
number *número (o)*

often *muitas vezes*
oil *óleo (o)*
OK *está bem*
old *velho/antigo*
olive oil *azeite (o)*
on foot *a pé*
on Saturdays *aos sábados*
on the left *à esquerda*
on the right *à direita*
open *aberto*
opportunity *oportunidade (a)*
oranges *laranjas (as)*
others *outros/as*
outside *fora*

packet *pacote (o)*
parents *pais (os)*
passer-by *transeunte (o/a)*

passport *passaporte (o)*
pears *pêras (as)*
people *gente (a)/pessoas (as)*
per night *por noite*
personally *pessoalmente*
petrol *gasolina (a)*
picture *quadro (o)*
pill *comprimido (o)*
plastic *plástico*
platform *linha (a)*
please *por favor*
pleased to meet you *muito prazer*
pollution *poluição (a)*
port *porto (o)*
Portuguese *português*
post office *correios (os)*
postcard *postal (o)*
pretty *bonito/lindo*
price *preço (o)*
probably *provavelmente*
problem *problema (o)*

quite *bastante*

ruin *obras (a)*
reception *recepção (a)*
region *região (a)*
reserved *reservado*
return (ticket) *ida e volta*
right there *ali mesmo*
road *rua (a)*
road signs *sinais (os)*
room *quarto (o)*

s/he eats *come*
s/he prefers *prefere*
sandwich *sanduíche (o)*
s/he says *diz*
school *escola (a)*
seafood *mariscos (os)*
s/he sells *vende*
shirt *camisa (a)*
shoes *sapatos (os)*
shop *loja (a)*
single (ticket) *ida (a)*
sister *irmã (a)*
size *tamanho (o)*
skirt *saia (a)*
small *pequeno*
smoked ham *presunto (o)*
snow *neve (a)*
so then *então*

soap-operas *telenovelas (as)*
social club *clube (o)*
soft drink *refrigerante (o)*
sometimes *de vez em quando*
son *filho (o)*
Spain *Espanha (a)*
Spanish *espanhol*
spicy *picante*
square *praça (a)*
stamp *selo (o)*
station *estação (a)*
student *estudante (o/a)*
style *estilo (o)*
suitcase *mala (a)*
summer *verão (o)*
surname *sobrenome (o)*
swimming pool *piscina (a)*
syrup, cough mixture *xarope (o)*

table *mesa (a)*
taxi *táxi (o)*
teacher *professor/a*
television *televisão (a)*
thank goodness! *ainda bem!*
thank you *obrigado/a*
that *esse/aquele*
that, which *que*
then, after *depois*
there *ali/lá*
there is, are *há*
thing *coisa (a)*
third *terceiro*
this *este, esta*
ticket *bilhete (o)*
to ask for *pedir*
to buy *comprar*
to change *trocar/cambiar*
to come *vir*
to feel *sentir-se*
to fill *encher*
to fill in *preencher*
to get to know *conhecer*
to get, catch *pegar*
to go *ir*
to improve *melhorar*
to leave *partir/deixar*
to listen to *escutar*
to paint *pintar*
to pass/spend *passar*
to play *jogar/brincar/tocar*

to put *pôr*
to reserve *reservar*
to see, watch *ver*
to sit down *sentar-se*
to stay *ficar*
to swim *nadar*
to take *tomar/levar*
to try, taste *provar/experimentar*
to work *trabalhar*
today *hoje*
town, city *cidade (a)*
trousers *calças (as)*
typical *típico*
typically *tipicamente*

underneath *debaixo*
university *universidade (a)*
until, up to *até*

various *vários*
very *muito*
very well *muito bem*
view *vista (a)*

wallet, purse *carteira (a)*
s/he wants *quer*
waterfalls *cataratas (as)*
welcome *bem-vindo/a*
well *bem*
well then *então*
what do you do? *o que faz?*
what else? *que mais?*
what is it like? *como é?*
where are you from? *de onde é?*
which? *qual?*
who *quem?*
wife *esposa/mulher (a)*
wind *vento (o)*
window *janela (a)*
wine *vinho (o)*
with *com*
without *sem*
wonderful *maravilhoso*
world *mundo (o)*

years *anos (os)*
yes *sim*
yesterday *ontem*
you can *pode*

grammar index

Verbs

	Unit
commands	7
conditional	13
future	7, 13
haver	4, 8, 16, 17
imperfect	17
passive voice	10
past participles	13
pluperfect	18
present tense	2, 5
preterite	15
progressive tenses	6, 13
reflexive verbs	2
regular verbs	2, 5
ser/estar/ficar	1, 2, 3
spelling changes	8, 15
subjunctive	18
ter	2, 8, 13

Grammar

adjectives	1, 2, 5, 6, 12, 15, 17
adverbs	15
articles (the, a)	1
cada	16
contractions	2, 4
demonstratives	1, 4, 13
exclamations	13, 16
forms of address	1

teach® yourself

Afrikaans
Arabic
Arabic Script, Beginner's
Bengali
Brazilian Portuguese
Bulgarian
Cantonese
Catalan
Chinese
Chinese, Beginner's
Chinese Language, Life & Culture
Chinese Script, Beginner's
Croatian
Czech
Danish
Dutch
Dutch, Beginner's
Dutch Dictionary
Dutch Grammar
English, American (EFL)
English as a Foreign Language
English, Correct
English Grammar
English Grammar (EFL)
English, Instant, for French Speakers
English, Instant, for German Speakers
English, Instant, for Italian Speakers
English, Instant, for Spanish Speakers
English for International Business
English Language, Life & Culture
English Verbs
English Vocabulary
Finnish
French
French, Beginner's
French Grammar
French Grammar, Quick Fix
French, Instant
French, Improve your
French Language, Life & Culture
French Starter Kit
French Verbs

French Vocabulary
Gaelic
Gaelic Dictionary
German
German, Beginner's
German Grammar
German Grammar, Quick Fix
German, Instant
German, Improve your
German Language, Life & Culture
German Verbs
German Vocabulary
Greek
Greek, Ancient
Greek, Beginner's
Greek, Instant
Greek, New Testament
Greek Script, Beginner's
Gulf Arabic
Hebrew, Biblical
Hindi
Hindi, Beginner's
Hindi Script, Beginner's
Hungarian
Icelandic
Indonesian
Irish
Italian
Italian, Beginner's
Italian Grammar
Italian Grammar, Quick Fix
Italian, Instant
Italian, Improve your
Italian Language, Life & Culture
Italian Verbs
Italian Vocabulary
Japanese
Japanese, Beginner's
Japanese, Instant
Japanese Language, Life & Culture
Japanese Script, Beginner's
Korean

Latin
Latin American Spanish
Latin, Beginner's
Latin Dictionary
Latin Grammar
Nepali
Norwegian
Panjabi
Persian, Modern
Polish
Portuguese
Portuguese, Beginner's
Portuguese Grammar
Portuguese, Instant
Portuguese Language, Life & Culture
Romanian
Russian
Russian, Beginner's
Russian Grammar
Russian, Instant
Russian Language, Life & Culture
Russian Script, Beginner's
Sanskrit
Serbian
Spanish
Spanish, Beginner's
Spanish Grammar
Spanish Grammar, Quick Fix
Spanish, Instant
Spanish, Improve your
Spanish Language, Life & Culture
Spanish Starter Kit
Spanish Verbs
Spanish Vocabulary
Swahili
Swahili Dictionary
Swedish
Tagalog
Teaching English as a Foreign Language
Teaching English One to One
Thai
Turkish
Turkish, Beginner's
Ukrainian
Urdu
Urdu Script, Beginner's
Vietnamese
Welsh
Welsh Dictionary
Welsh Language, Life & Culture
Xhosa
Zulu

available from bookshops and on-line retailers